From the mind of author Randall Brooks, the author of such fictional works as *The Two Worlds of the Mind, Conversations at the Party,* and *The Maze,* comes a scathing non-fiction book taking on things like politics and religion, to grammar rules, film remakes, and how children are raised in today's society.

Written with vibrant wit and biting satire, and sometimes flat-out dead-on serious about some issues of today, this is a book that anyone concerned with today's world should read.

So, without further ado, let the "ranting & raving" commence!

By Randall Brooks

Novels ~
The Two Worlds of the Mind
Von Wyck: The Complete Story by Victor Holocaust
Brent's World

Short Story Collections ~
Conversations at the Party
Perfect Strangers
The Maze
Erotomania

Non-fiction ~
The De Palma Rant
Random Film Reviews
Random Reviews II: Music & Books

Lyrics ~
Von Wyck Songbook Volume 1: 1986 - 1988
Von Wyck Songbook Volume 2: 1988 - 1991
Von Wyck Songbook Volume 3: 1991 - 1997
Von Wyck Songbook Volume 4: 1998 - 2011

Covering everything from religion, politics, grammar rules, child-rearing, and thoughts on film remakes…

RANTING & RAVING

RANDALL BROOKS

RANTING & RAVING
Copyright Randall Brooks 2014
ISBN 978-1500675707

First Printing, July 2014

Amazon Publishing has allowed this work to remain exactly as the author intended, verbatim, without editorial input.

RANTING & RAVING

An essay on politics, Christianity, grammar rules, child rearing, and even thoughts on film remakes divided into four sections.

A non-fiction rant about homosexuality, Christianity, politics, and the ignorance of the world...

ABOMINATIONS

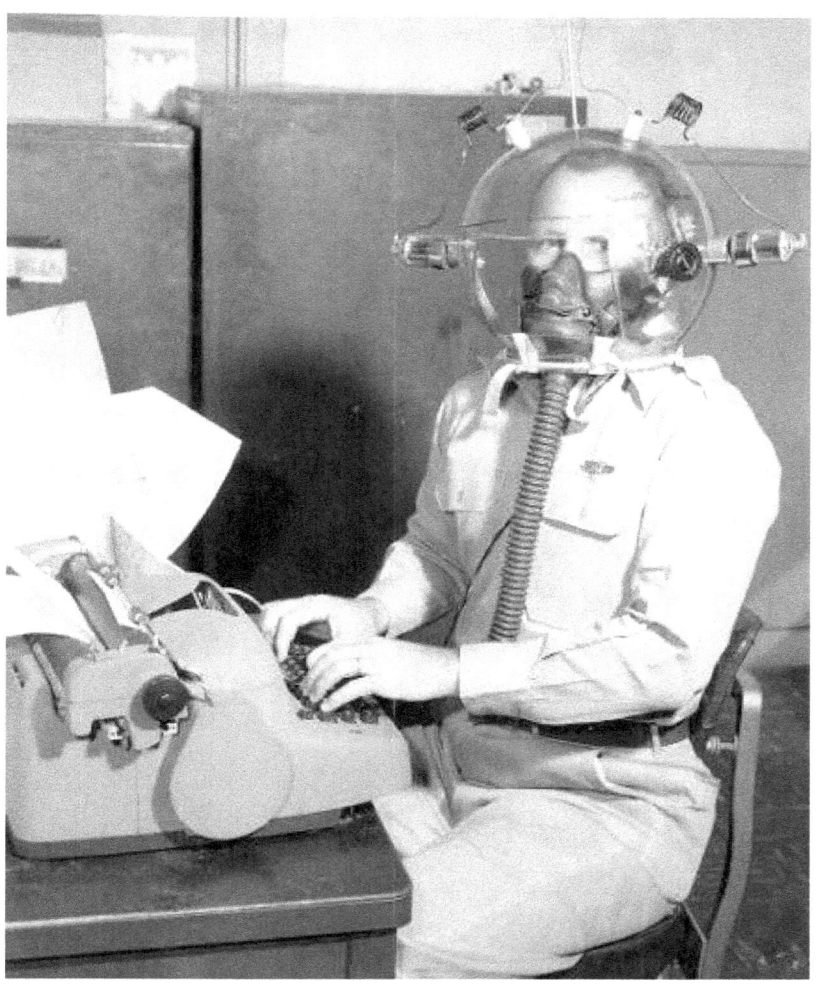

Nothing like politics, religion or sexuality comments to get people emotional to the point that they lose all logic!

The *Duck Dynasty* patriarch Phil Robertson has recently been taken off of the show indefinitely following some "Hate For Jesus" remarks he made, in which he suggested that the whole of the LGBT community is an abomination to God.

Predictably, every single right wing media outlet, politicians, and pretty well every single person in America who finds themselves unable to count to three without starting over at least twice has jumped on the Phil Robertson bandwagon.

Let me just say that I had no interest what-so-ever in *Duck Dynasty* or any of the people from "DD" *before* all the "drama" surrounding *Duck Dynasty*. Just saying. You know, even if I was the type of person to be anti-gay, I *still* wouldn't want to align myself with the likes of someone like Phil Robertson. He has to be the most backward, primitive, closest-thing-to-a-caveman, ignorant person I've laid eyes on in a long time.

I sure do hope people don't make the mistake of confusing "good ole boys" with rednecks like Robertson. A redneck and a good ole boy are about as different as night and day! Good ole boys are good hearted, open minded, decent individuals who just like to be who they are and are accepting of everyone as long as people are polite, respectful, and accepting of them.

However, rednecks are close minded, ignorant, and hate pretty much everyone and everything different than themselves.

People are making me sick with their "Bring Back Phil Robertson" posts. Most of the people posting that crap have never made a "stand" for anything on the internet. Yep, great time to stand up for something you believe in. Or it's the same sad bunch of people who made some kind of lame stand for Chik-Fil-A! I love how we refer to hate as faith. Wow. Amazing.

Yes, there is something wrong with it, because when someone says that two people of the same sex loving one another is a "sin", then when some violent hate crime is committed and someone is killed or tortured for being gay, the person who committed the hideous crime can then say, well it's in the Bible that it's wrong, and I was just acting on my Christian faith.

For anyone who may not understand why some people are so upset over people defending the *Duck Dynasty* redneck for his ignorant opinions, let me try to make this clear for you:

It is people like him (and you if you support him) that help spread hate, intolerance, prejudice and bigotry, and then when someone is killed or tortured because of their sexuality, it only helps encourage the people who do such hideous crimes.

It really shouldn't be that hard to understand or comprehend why it is wrong to have such backward, primitive, dangerous views, and even more wrong to say them in public and expect to have others support you.

And to make matters worse, there is such an outpouring of support for this idiot from Internet trolls, saying how his freedom of speech has been taken away (because he was fired from his job, you know, like any other employee gets fired when an employer is dissatisfied with them), and how he is someone who has such strong "Biblical principles". Make me gag already. We can not as a nation continue to allow people to spread ignorance and intolerance.

Another thing about the *Duck Dynasty* guy is that he is making stuff up and trying to attribute it to Bible Scripture, which is not only dangerous, but blasphemous, and turns lots of people who don't know better against the Christian religion. Just something to think about.

Why doesn't this duck brain give a speech on the sin of being rich or greed? Why isn't he against drunks? Unlike homosexuality, the Bible has plenty of condemnation for those things. But he wouldn't would he, for that would mean condemn himself.

If some people in this nation don't pull their head out of their ass and stop attacking poor people, homosexuals, black people, and/or anyone different than them, then we are heading in the same direction as Nazi Germany did. Just something to think about.

Loving the rich, hating on the poor, blacks and the gays will get you though the pearly gates! Hopefully via a cannon blast. Welcome to 'Merica. Priorities. Some of ours suck.

What next, are people going to start going after overweight people, saying how it's in the Bible that it's a sin to overeat, and how gluttony is wrong, and that God hates fat people?! Seriously, it's that stupid!

To all the Bible illiterate people who go around hollering "It's in the Bible", here's a little lesson for you: Over the centuries people who misunderstood or misinterpreted the Bible have done terrible things. The Bible has been misused to defend bloody crusades and tragic inquisitions; to support slavery, apartheid, and segregation; to persecute Jews and other non-Christian people of faith; to support Hitler's Third Reich and the Holocaust; to oppose medical science; to condemn interracial marriage; to execute women as witches; and to support the Ku Klux Klan.

I tell you all something, all these so-called Christians going around spewing hateful bigoted prejudiced remarks and then declaring it's because it's in the Bible, and they are defending their faith, well, it makes people cringe whenever they hear/see the word "Christian", and it drives them away from the *real* Christian faith. Just something to think about.

The people who want to bring up the Old Testament of the Bible as their code of living, well you need to live by the whole Bible, not just the parts you like:

1. Women should be treated as 2nd class citizens.
2. Get a divorce and get stoned to death! No exceptions!
3. All disobedient children must be put to death. No favoritism shown here either!
4. If you get raped then you must marry your rapist or be branded a sinner!
5. Everyone should own at least 2 slaves!
6. No eating pork or you'll burn in Hell! No lie!

I have studied the Bible extensively over the years, and there is no point in the Bible that Jesus mentions homosexuals at all. And if you mean where he mentions eunochs, well, that is another story altogether. But, since some people have brought up Matthew, and want to assess to Him talking about homosexuality, they might want to read it closer, because He clearly says "There are those that are made that way by other men, those that have made themselves that way, and those that are born that way, and there are many who won't understand."

I love it when I tell some so-called "Christian" that I am a Bible scholar, and I quote stuff directly from the Bible, and they *still* want to argue and try to say I am wrong. No it's not me that's wrong, it's your ill-advised interpretation of the Holy Word. True story.

In the New Testament, Jesus Christ never said one word about homosexuality. Never. Not one word. He did speak about the evil of greed, how we should help the helpless, feed the poor, and love one another as we love ourselves, and do unto others as we would have them do unto ourselves.

Oh, and by the way, Phil Robertson didn't just quote from the Bible, he *misquoted* from the Bible.

Well, his beliefs are wrong and hurtful, and A&E have the right to fire him over it. There is no freedom of speech being taken away here. If you think so, then next time at your job, walk in and start talking about how much you hate gay people, black people, and think women should be in the kitchen and not open their mouths, and see if that doesn't get you fired.

Yet one more attempt to try to explain to some people who obviously don't "get" it why there is so much uproar over the speech made from the idiot from *Duck Dynasty*:

Homosexuality is not a "sin". It is not "wrong" for someone to be homosexual. There is nothing "deviant" about it. So, for some idiot to try to lump it in with prostitution and/or bestiality and say that God will punish people for being that way, well, *that* is wrong, and it is also dangerous hate speech, because it feeds right into the mentality of people who go out and commit hate crimes against homosexual people, because they can then say, "Well, I've heard it's in the Bible that it's a sin, and I was just acting on my faith."

See how that works?

But, the difference between religion and homosexuality is religion is a *choice*, and homosexuality isn't. It's also not a "preference", but simply a sexual orientation.

And sorry if some people feel that it's been thrown in their face, but again, unless you are a gay person yourself, then you have no clue what it's like being a gay person and having heterosexual shit thrown in your face day in and day out, 24/7, and all we want is equality, not any special favors.

Being a Christian is a *choice*. Picking a political party is a *choice*. Being homophobic is a *choice*. Being homosexual is *not* a choice. See how that works?

It's insane how many people pick and choose the parts of the Bible they can use to justify their bigotry and ignore the other parts.

I don't follow the author of Leviticus nor the author of Romans (Paul was the worst thing to happen to the message of Christ). I follow Christ, who never condemned gay people. The same people who think Jesus condemned gay people also typically will not feed the hungry and think for-profit healthcare is a boon to the American economy.

This is what I have been trying to tell local yokels around here the past few days. The Old Testament is the History of Ancient Israel. Christians are to follow the teachings of Jesus Christ and the New Testament.

Now I'm finished discussing this issue. And from this point on, if I hear anyone making even a remote negative remark about homosexuality being a "sin" or "against God", or saying something like "I'll pray for them", or "we're all sinners", and/or showing support for the guy from DD, I won't hesitate to remove them from my life.

I tolerate *lots* of stuff, but I do not tolerate anyone trying to make someone else feel bad about who they are. It's no different than disliking someone because of their skin color or their size.

I'm telling people right now, I don't care how close or how distant friends we are, or if you're someone I know in the real world or someone I met online, or if you're family, if anyone supports the guy from *Duck Dynasty*, please remove yourself from my life now. Or I will do it for you when I find out your stance on things.

I am a 47 year old openly gay man, and I will not tolerate having anyone in my life that thinks that I am some kind of "deviant" or "sinner" because or my sexual orientation.

No offense to anyone, but do some people really think that a gay man in his late 40's has never heard all this shit before? That he has not ever bothered to look stuff up in the Bible and seen what was there and what wasn't? That he hasn't delved into studying all the different translations and interpretations?

That he hasn't had these same arguments and debates with other people over the years? That they are the first people to say this shit to him? That this is the first that he is ever hearing about it?

Please! Buy yourself a clue! Thank you!

You know, one of the main reasons I didn't want to get into anything political or "issue" related on some social internet sites is because I've learned that when you do something like that (you know, speak out about something you may be a little "passionate" about, or try to tell someone the *truth*), the very same people who are crying out that they are having their freedom of speech taken away from them and are such (alleged) devout advocates of free speech are the very same one's who have hit the "delete friend" button.

Funny how someone on the left will be tolerant of *lots* of things that people on the right say, but the moment the person on the left starts voicing their opinion, the people on the right start yelling how they're offended and want to shut the person on the left up.
So nice to see how mature they really are.

That is the whole problem, they only want to talk, they never want to listen. If they listened they might change their minds, and that is just too scary for them.

Oddly enough it's mainly been people that I went to high school with, even though I didn't know them in high school. And even though they post almost daily about how they feel strongly about something the right is saying, and even has made opposing comments on some things I've posted, trying to challenge my view, and I've always replied in kind; but when I start posting stuff from the left view, whoa, that's a race of a different color to them, and next thing I notice that they are no longer on my friend list.

It's so funny, really. I'm friends with people from all parts of the world on the internet, so does someone really think I'm going to stress over something some backward local yokel thinks. Seriously.

I hate that I forget and have to remind myself so many times that you cannot fight ignorance; it will beat you down and wear you out every time. Something that I hate to the point that it makes my fucking blood boil is when I see idiots saying shit like: Oh, I hate when homosexuals throw it in our face!

Well, here's a very true story for those fucking morons: No one is throwing anything in your fucking face! But, I've got something I'd like to throw in your face and tell you to open up and say "ah"!

And this isn't an attack on anyone, nor is it an attack on Christians, so for anyone to feel that way is stupid. The only people being attacked are bigots and people who are openly expressing hostility and prejudice towards others. And now they are crying that they feel their freedom of speech is being taken away because more and more people are sick and tired of hearing their rhetoric. It makes me laugh!

And as for Phil Roberts being fired over what he said, there is more than just the one incident where he has made some very nasty comments about how he feels homosexuals are sinners who deserve the wrath of God, so you figure out if that means he thinks they should be put to death or not, because I surely understand it to mean that. People need to start checking on things before they get all riled up and try to take sides with an issue, and when they do they will more than likely realize there is a history of more than one occasion where the guilty party has done bad behavior and is now finally being exposed for it.

And, for your information, Phil had the right to free speech, he practiced that right, he spoke, and he also has the right to suffer backlash from the public since he is a public figure.

And A&E also have the right to fire his bigoted ass just like any other employer has to fire an employee they are dissatisfied with. Wow, the stupid in this county burns!

I'm 47 years old, and it's blowing my mind. I thought this shit ended way back in the 80's!

On another note I am also glad of the whole DD incident because it has given opportunity to have some very *interesting* conversations with some people with differing views and opinions, and some very enlightening things have been said, which I've enjoyed and appreciate.

And some people have falsely accused me of not liking it when people disagree with me, what bullocks!

Hey, a good example of how the right wing only speak out when it's for someone else on the right being attacked for expressing bigoted remarks, is Alec Baldwin being fired from his TV gig for calling some asshole reporter a fag because the guy was hounding Alec trying to get a photo of him and his daughter, and Alec snapped and told the guy off and called him a fag in the process. But notice you don't hear a *peep* from the Republican right about that incident.

And, honestly, I would support Alec getting his job back! It wasn't like he went into an interview and started spewing a bunch of Archaic backward ignorant bigoted stuff, you know, like Phil Robertson did.

I think he actually called him a "Drama Queen" or something of that nature. But see Alec is a Democrat so they don't give a shit that he lost his job for a similar reason.

But it really wasn't too similar, because what Alec did wasn't really that bad, all he did was snap and go off on someone for harassing him, unlike making some blatant interview. But either way, unless it happens to a Republican, they don't give a crap.

Well, just like with the Dixie Chicks, who simply said during a concert that they were ashamed that

President Bush was from the same state (Texas) they live in, and the right wing went off, burning their CD's, calling for a nationwide boycott, wanting to run them out of the country, practically ruining their career, saying shit like "How dare they disrespect our President!"

And now those same people are the one's speaking the loudest against President Obama, calling him everything but the Devil himself, wanting to impeach him, calling him "Obummer", disrespecting him in every way possible; but it's alright when they do it!

The right wing went nuts when Natalie Maines spoke her mind so why can't people with a differing opinion do the same?

Oh, and by the way, where is the outcry from the right wing for support for Alec Baldwin being fired over something very similar? Oh that's right, I don't see it.

Alec got fired from his TV gig a couple weeks ago for a very similar incident, and *no one* from the right even said as much as "Boo!" Just saying.

I'm still waiting for someone to come out and defend Alec. Maybe I should be the first and try to get some kind of GIVE ALEC BALDWIN HIS JOB BACK campaign. Anyone with me?

You know, I just realized something, it's so messed up that as long as someone is ranting about being hardcore Conservative Republican, it is alright, and almost welcomed by all, but as soon as someone remotely hints at being Liberal Democrat, oh my god, watch out, the pitchforks come out and the name calling begins!

Seriously, what is up with that?

I guess the problem is, straight people are so fucking used to saying shit that offends people and not having someone call them on it, and when they do they get all damn bent out of shape and defensive and want to attack us for defending ourselves.

But Phil Robertson was not asked about his views on homosexuality - he was asked, "What, in your mind, is sinful?" He didn't respond with murder or rape or child abuse or the greed of the wealthy while others live in poverty, he responded with gay people. That disturbs me.

As research would appear to suggest that sexuality isn't as black-and-white as "straight-or-gay", and that sexuality is actually a fluid and constantly fluctuating spectrum, it stands to reason that those who spend their lives worrying about homosexuality are more inclined to find themselves aroused by it. This would stand to explain all those fire-and-brimstone homophobic preachers caught having sex with men or boys, and why anal sex is so important to homophobes.

First of all, it's not a lifestyle. I can guarantee you that Anderson Cooper, Billie Jean King and myself all live vastly different lifestyles. I'm not sure which parts of that gay lifestyle you disagree with. Using the phrase "gay lifestyle" diminishes the reality of people who are lesbian or gay.

Name calling is different from labeling. First of all, if you truly are anti-gay, being called a homophobe wouldn't be an insult. Just as I'm sure KKK members aren't bothered being called racist. And yes, it's the same thing. Homophobia, specifically the effects of it, kills thousands every year and leaves thousands others homeless. It is our responsibility as a community, and especially those of us who have been able to build safety structures against homophobia, to call out hatred and homophobia where we see it, label it, and hold people accountable who perpetuate it.

Dear Phil (duck dynasty) Robertson,

Thank you for doing so much to educate people regarding God's Law. I have learned a great deal from your show, and I try to share that knowledge with as many people as I can. When someone tries to defend the homosexual lifestyle, for example, I simply remind him that Leviticus 18:22 clearly states it to be an abomination. End of debate.

I do need some advice from you, however, regarding some of the specific laws and how to best follow them.

a) When I burn a bull on the altar as a sacrifice, I know it creates a pleasing odor for the Lord (Lev 1:9). The problem is my neighbors. They claim the odor is not pleasing to them. Should I smite them?

b) I would like to sell my daughter into

slavery, as sanctioned in Exodus 21:7.
In this day and age, what do you think
would be a fair price for her?

c) I know that I am allowed no contact
with a woman while she is in her
period of menstrual uncleanliness (Lev
15:19-24). The problem is, how do I
tell? I have tried asking, but most
women take offense.

d) Lev. 25:44 states that I may indeed
possess slaves, both male and female,
provided they are purchased from
neighboring nations. A friend of mine
claims that this applies to Mexicans,
but not Canadians. Can you clarify?
Why can't I own Canadians?

e) I have a neighbor who insists on
working on the Sabbath. Exodus 35:2
clearly states he should be put to death.
Am I morally obligated to kill him
myself?

f) A friend of mine feels that even though
eating shellfish is an abomination (Lev
11:10), it is a lesser abomination than
homosexuality. I don't agree. Can you
settle this?

g) Lev 21:20 states that I may not
approach the altar of God if I have a
defect in my sight. I have to admit that I
wear reading glasses. Does my vision

have to be 20/20, or is there some wiggle room here?

h) Most of my male friends get their hair trimmed, including the hair around their temples, even though this is expressly forbidden by Lev 19:27. How should they die?

i) I know from Lev 11:6-8 that touching the skin of a dead pig makes me unclean, but may I still play football if I wear gloves?

j) My uncle has a farm. He violates Lev 19:19 by planting two different crops in the same field, as does his wife by wearing garments made of two different kinds of thread (cotton/polyester blend). He also tends to curse and blaspheme a lot. Is it really necessary that we go to all the trouble of getting the whole town together to stone them? (Lev 24:10-16) Couldn't we just burn them to death at a private family affair like we do with people who sleep with their in-laws? (Lev. 20:14)

I know you have studied these things extensively, so I am confident you can help. Thank you again for reminding us that God's word is eternal and unchanging.

Signed: Your devoted disciple and adoring fan.

Phil Robertson... Couple more points:

1) Be a homophobe. Just don't use the Bible to justify your idiotic opinions. Unless that is, you also believe slavery is okay, rude children should be put to death (alongside people who work on Saturday) and women are inferior to men.
And maybe you do agree with those points too. Just don't pick and choose what parts of the Bible you want to take literally.

2) Free Speech is free to everyone. That includes A&E, advertisers and the public. They get to choose if they want someone like Mr. homophobe Phil Robertson on their station.

3) We're better than this as a country. Let's embrace our differences.
For example, wearing camouflage and blowing into a plastic device while trying to kill ducks sounds like my equivalent to Hell....but I don't judge you Mr. Phil Robertson!

Upon hearing Phil Robertson's views on gays, I try to focus on the struggles of the gay children that are growing up in rural America and how we as adults make their lives harder or easier. They don't need someone popularizing the condemnation of gays. The Bible condemns and prohibits a lot of things that we all do every day, such as wearing a polyblend shirt: Leviticus 19:19: Do not wear clothing woven of two kind of material.

I support everyone's right to free speech! However, we all know that historically there has been speech such as Mein Kampf that cannot be supported in any way because it is hate speech: "the personification of the Devil is the symbol of all evil assumes the living shape of the Jew."

I am puzzled that some people don't see Phil Robertson's condemnation of gays and his suggestion that homosexuality is a step away from bestiality as qualifying as hate speech. In 1899, in Tallulah, Louisiana, three Italian American shopkeepers were lynched because they had given equal status in their shops to blacks. A vigilante mob hanged five Italian Americans, the three shopkeepers and two bystanders. If people back then could stand up for equality at the risk of being lynched, I would think that almost 115 years later, we could at least agree that Phil Robertson using the Bible to condemn millions of people cannot be tolerated because it is hate speech.

The great doctrine 'All men are created equal' that is incorporated into the Declaration of Independence by Thomas Jefferson was paraphrased from the writing of Philip Mazzei, an Italian-born patriot and pamphleteer who was a close friend of Jefferson. The truth of the matter is that all of our ancestors fought for equality and not just their own. Since we stand on the shoulders of those who fought for us, the least we can do to honor them is to continue to fight for freedom and equality.

I believe this entire saga is nothing more than a publicity stunt to get more viewers to the show. It was too well orchestrated, too well timed and too well publicized. I believe that Mr. Robertson knew exactly what he was doing and he positively knew that his comments would start an uproar. Just a stunt.

And, if not to make matters worse, there are tons of memes flooding Internet sites, trying to bring (and compare) President Obama into all of this mess.

This has to be the biggest bunch of ignorant bullshit I've seen on the Internet in my life! What the fuck does the incident with Phil Roberts have to do with President Obama?! Wow!

Told you, the stupid in this country burns!

Instead of worrying about the homerseshuals, why don't we try to do something about the pill epidemic that is sweeping the nation?!

I've said before and I'll say again, even though I don't like getting into politics, what this country so badly needs are some fiscal Conservative/socially Liberal politicians in office.

There are a lot of right wing Republicans in office these days, and that is one of the biggest problems in this nation. Right wing people are more socially conservative obsessed. They take little fragments of the Bible that suit their warped agenda and then whack people over the head with it, so to speak.

Stop with the "freedom of speech" arguments already. This dumb redneck's freedom of speech has not been violated; if it had, he'd be locked up in jail. Read the constitution: The freedom of speech clause does not mean "freedom from consequences for what you say".

By turning it into a Free Speech issue, they are able to completely avoid the unabashed bigotry of the content of the message...right along with all of their Free Speech supporters. I think we all know what they are really supporting.

What kills me is when people on the right say how they want people to be tolerant of them, and allow them to have free speech, but the minute someone from the left speaks out about something, they put their hands over the ears and start shouting, "La-la-la-la" like a little kid.

See, people on the right only want freedom of speech as long as you're agreeing with them. But the minute you say something they don't agree with, they want to silence you.

That's really what this is all about,, the right wing are finally being exposed for being hateful prejudiced bigots, and they can't take it, and are crying that they are having their freedoms taken away from them, when the *only* "freedom" being taken away is people are no longer tolerating their ignorant backward bigoted views.

And if I may: Gay people have been persecuted for years, for centuries, for motherfucking millennia.

Really persecuted, primarily by people of faith. And our persecution didn't take the form of straight people wishing us well but failing to use precisely the right phrase. No, we were burned at the stake, arrested, imprisoned, committed, lobotomized, thrown out of our homes, and fired from our jobs; our children were taken from us, our partners were barred from our hospital rooms during medical emergencies, and on and on and on.

By the way, the persecution of gay people by people of faith continues: Gay sex was re-criminalized in India last week after a coalition of Muslim and Christian organizations, among others, asked the Indian Supreme Court to overturn a lower court ruling that had legalized consensual gay sex. People will go to prison.

And seriously, of *all* the bad things that have happened in this world, like slavery, wars, lynching people, killing people because they were different, burning people alive because they were allegedly "witches", do you *really* think that God is going to judge someone for loving someone else of the same sex? Buy a clue.

What is wrong with humans?! Every time there has been someone step forth to try to lead us down a path of peace, acceptance, love, and tolerance they have been assassinated and/or crucified?! Just something to think about.

And here's another truth that may shock you: All of these people with a mob mentality that want to do away with, burn alive, lynch, kill anyone different than them (you know, Jewish, black, gay," witches", etc etc) are the same type people who crucified Christ.

Yep....it starts out with "words" and ends up with crap like this. Has anybody ever heard of a little thing called Nazi Germany? It started with a few people spewing hate and ignorance...and well we see how that turned out. That is why we have to have ZERO tolerance, people. We have to nip it...nip it in the bud!!

If people can't learn to accept each others' differences and appreciate the fact that we are all different and unique, then it will be a very sad world to live in. True story.

A non-fiction essay about how in 2014 people are still having to fight for equality…

The Battle Rages On…

I.

"Does it make me homophobic because I don't want a man's penis in my mouth?" ;)

You know, I don't know a single gay person who thinks and/or talks about gay sex as much as any of the Right Wing bunch do. True story. I mean, they put an awful *lot* of thought into it, if you know what I mean!

Why is Christianity so annoyingly obsessed with homosexuality? Even if you accept that the Bible denounces homosexual behavior as sinful, what makes the Bible's purportedly anti-gay message so special that modern day Christians still cling for dear life to its tenuous existence?

The passages related to gay sex are no more numerous or emphasized than Bible passages condemning countless other behaviors that we now see as acceptable. People pick and choose what parts of the Bible to believe.

Why do intelligent humans in the year 2014 still believe homosexuality is a sin? I'm a Christian, I've read the Bible, and yes before you all pounce on me and ask me what the Bible says about Homosexuality, I would remind you that the reality is, it was written by *men*. Men who had absolutely no understanding of homosexuality. Men who feared what they didn't understand.

Because sadly, many congregations are fed the concept that "believing in the Lord and this laundry list of bigoted things that have nothing really to do with Jesus or his teachings at all makes you better than other people."

They cling to their bigotry because they really do believe they are better than other people, when God is supposed to love everyone equally. They see it being disproven/debunked, and it throws them into a state of existential panic ("but we're supposed to be better than everyone else! My preacher told me so!")- so they cling to it all the harder even as more and more people are starting to wake up and realize it is the word of man, not of God.

You can't just pick and choose what you believe from the Bible. I would say, brothers and sisters, use your common sense. Don't spend your life brain washed by the Church. Jesus is so much bigger than your religiosity.

I honestly can't believe I am having to even have these type discussions/debates at my age. I thought this "fight" was fought (and won) many, many, many years ago. It literally astounds me to see that the issue of homosexuality is even a topic of debate anymore, especially a topic to be targeted by bigoted, prejudiced and hateful people.

But, believe it or not, here it is 2014, and here we are still defending ourselves against lesser minded cretins on the planet.

What continues to boggle my mind about homophobes, racists and the like is the mindset of "You living your life suppresses *my* right to oppress you. Free speech for me! My First Amendment! I share your pain!" And they don't get the doublethink in that, or the irony.

Do you realize that gay people have been in existence since the beginning of time? They didn't just pop up in the 2000's. If being gay is a choice, then I want you to come visit me. I'll will take you to a gay bar. You will wave the magic wand or whatever gay people use to become gay, and you will choose to be gay for one night. You can make out with a man and have sex with him. Then, the next day, you can choose to be straight again. If you can't choose to be gay in that bar, then being gay is not a choice.

Please allow me to clarify: 1. Yes. gay men and women *are* born that way. 2. There is nothing *wrong* with being born that way. 3. It's *way beyond* time this is accepted in our society, and our assistance to youngsters struggling with their identity is to *support* them and encourage them to be who they are and who they want to be.

Jesus never mentioned homosexuality. In fact, "homosexual" wasn't a word in the bible until 1946. Before that, the majority referenced "sodomite" as an indicator that Jesus was referring to sexuality, which was an erroneous assumption based on a translation from a part of the bible describing what happened to the angels in Sodom.

In the original texts, there was no mention of homosexuality at all. The premise for the argument that there was a reference is based on a single Greek word, one used in other areas of the Greek texts, by Jesus, to describe such things as fabric. Jesus was the deciding factor, and he said to love unconditionally, and to live without judgement.

You know, what bothered me the most about the whole Phil Robertson fiasco, was that people were saying how he was quoting the Bible, and I wanted to scream at them, no he's not, he's misquoting it!

It kills me when I have to go round and round with idiots like that, especially because they don't seem to comprehend that I have closely studied pretty much every aspect of the Bible, trying to find what it says on particular subjects - especially the subject of homosexuality.

Seriously, you have people asking people online to "like" to support Phil Robertson's right to believe in the Bible?! No one was trying to take away his right to believe in the Bible! What some people were upset over, however, was him using false Scripture (you know, comparable to using the Lord's name in vain) to help spread his agenda of hate and bigotry. Something that Jesus Christ would not tolerate.

People who are anti-gay are just the same as people who are prejudiced against black people, and I don't tolerate hate or bigotry or prejudice of any kind.

Not valuing someone else's love for their significant other as much as you would want your relationship valued is disrespectful. If you think your religion wants you to be disrespectful you either misunderstand your religion or you need a new one.

Well, that to me is the same thing as saying that black people should go back to using separate water fountains and sitting in the back of the bus. Oh, and it's not a "lifestyle" but a *sexual orientation*. People are born gay, so it's not like it's a disease or something you can catch, or something to be afraid of or grossed out by.

"Hate" is a poor choice of words. There are some who do hate us. But mostly we are misunderstood and feared, And I'm not talking about the kind of fear you get when you see a grizzly bear. I'm talking about fear of the unknown. You have been told repeatedly that the American family is in the toilet. You see same-gender marriage as being a part of that destruction.

Maybe you see opposite-gender marriage as a sort of "members only" club that you don't want to share. It's hard to tell what some of you think.

Here's the thing... I'm assuming that most of you are married. And I will hazard a guess that your marriage has not been impacted in any way by the thousands (millions?) of same-gender marriage that has taken place here and around the world. *No one's* marriage can have that kind of impact on you or your family.

Also, it could be the fact that since most of you are male, you just don't understand how two guys could ever be attracted to one another. But it's been happening since ancient times. There are tons of theories as to why same-gender attraction takes place. Frankly, I don't know why. I only know that I've been attracted to other guys since I was a kid. Just like you had crushes on girls when you were a kid, I had crushes on guys.

I fought it with all of my might. I didn't want to be "that way". I prayed and begged for God to stop those feelings. By the time I was in my 20's I was an emotional wreck. I hated myself. I forced myself to date girls even though the idea of being with them intimately repulsed me the same way that you being with a guy would repulse you.

I finally stopped praying for God to change me and ask that His will be done. In that moment I had one of the most spiritual awakenings I've ever experienced. I felt God's presence. He left me knowing that He made me the way He made me; that He wanted me to be happy.

You don't have to believe me. I'm just trying to explain things to you.

How do you explain me? I grew up in rural Tennessee in the 1980s. Growing up, I never met a single gay person. I dated girls. I was actually quite popular with them! But as I realized my sexuality, I realized I just wasn't sexually attracted to women. I had no idea why. I liked girls in a friend sense, but wasn't at all physically attracted to them. I'm attracted to men. I have no idea why. It just is, just like your sexuality just is. I didn't even have a word for it. I had to look it up to even know what to call it.

Nothing we do is going to change how people are. The only thing that changes is how we treat people who are born that way. That's it. They're regular, normal people just like you and me with love, hope and dreams, a desire to go to school, get good grades, get a good job, and if they're so lucky, fall in love and settle down. Just like everyone else.

I really hate to get into something that is considered an "issue" of any kind, but I feel this must be said.

So, if you are the type of person who has some kind of "problem" with people being gay, and/or are bothered by them, and/or are grossed out by the thought of them, then please exit my life so I won't have to be around and exposed to your backward ignorant ways.

I really can't believe I'm even having to say something like this in this day and age, especially at my age.

Telling someone they should love someone who hates them for who they are is like telling someone who is bullied that they should love their bully.

We have became a country of judgmental hypocrites who cannot wait to force beliefs down each others' throat while condemning everyone to Hell.

It just amazes me that right wing, tea party, and so called Americans are against Freedoms. If you use religion to suppress freedoms, you are just like the Taliban. Part of being American is Freedom For All, not some. If you are not for gay marriage don't get gay married. If you try to deny gay marriage because of religion, not American at all.

I really have a problem with people assessing homosexuality as a "sin". I don't see how anyone expressing love for another person can be seen as a "sin". It just defies reasonable thinking.

The fact there is a link between the ignorant hate about blacks and gays spewed by the *Duck Dynasty* nut and a site about Jesus is so disturbing. It's not Christian to condone judging others and condemnation. Let he without sin cast the first stone. Jesus taught love and tolerance, slept with lepers and was friends with prostitutes. I don't think He would condone putting all gays on an island and blowing it up somehow. Some people rather twist the Bible to stand in judgment of others than use the Bible to find ways to love others, especially those they do not understand. Love is the Christian way...LOVE.

No, not all Christians are ridiculous, just the ones like these that I point out. And, yes, it opens them to being easy to judge when they make such blatant ignorant blanket statements like they do about a subject they know nothing about.

And, as I said before and I'll say again, it's not a "lifestyle", but a *sexual orientation*. Please educate yourself on this matter, people, before you keep embarrassing yourself by speaking out and showing your bigotry and intolerance and incompassion toward a group of people you have no basic understanding of.

And, if they want to keep bringing up their choice laws of the Bible to live by, like I have said before, why aren't they living by *all* of them instead of cherry picking the one that allows them to be a bigot toward people who are homosexual?

They are no different than a racist. Their bigotry toward homosexuals is the same as being racist toward someone of a different race. They are nothing but "false prophets who come in His name and speaketh lies" and a "anti-Christ". Hopefully one day they will find the true meaning of Christ.

I have more than answered some of their silly questions, and I have provided actual Scripture to back what I'm saying, and they still keep dancing around like a bug at a bonfire, so to speak.

And, they never answer a lot of the key points that were made, they just simply keep insisting how they were no longer laws (which was kind of my point, duh), yet they keep insisting that homosexuality is wrong and "sinful", not seeing how ironic and ignorant they are being. Wow.

I always find it so funny when people who profess to be a "Christian" and know so much about the Bible are faced with actual *facts* and Scripture from the Bible, they still cling to their bigoted views and try to claim that the person presenting the actual documented Scripture is wrong.

Again, wow.

And, seriously, how can anyone with half a brain say there is any kind of "war on Christianity" when all they have to do is turn on their television on any Saturday or Sunday morning and see that pretty much *every* station has some kind of religious programming on for almost half the day?!
Unless they mean the war created by the people on the right that are seeming more and more each day like the "Anti-Christ". I think that might be it.

There is no loss of freedom for Christians!

I am a 48 year old man who has been of the Christian faith pretty much all my life, so don't try to tell me there is some kind of war on Christians.

What is happening is people are sick and tired of people like you having such bigoted beliefs and trying to use religion and the Bible as your excuse. And you can't take it. Well, boo-hoo.

You think homosexuality is a sign of end times? Over the past decade our country and allies have bombed two countries into the dirt. By some estimates well over 100,000 Iraqi and Afghan people have been killed--with millions more injured and left homeless. *That* would be more of an "end of times" type of event, if you ask me.

Oh, I see, God didn't bring an end to the world when people were being burned alive, accused of being "witches", or when Germans were literally burning people in ovens during the Nazi reign, or when slavery was rampant in America, or worse, the genocide of Indians when this country was founded, but He is going to reign down Judgement because two people of the same sex show love and affection for each other?

Please explain to me why you think that even remotely makes sense. I'll wait.

It's amazing to me that we the people will look at violence on TV and in movies and we won't even bat an eye. However when two people love each-other or show affection (regardless of orientation) we all get our panties in a bunch and suddenly have an opinion. Let's all take a step back and re-evaluate our priorities and look at the real issues in this world.

Yes, one man kissed his boyfriend and it was caught on tape. How many TV shows, news reports, and movies show straight couples kissing? How many straight couples kiss and hold hands in public? Who is flaunting their lifestyle? Everywhere you look you see straight couples engaging in loving behavior.

Well, personally, I find straight affection nauseating, but I don't complain about it because if I want to see a movie or TV show pretty much all I'm going to see is straight couples. Rarely will I see a lesbian or gay couple, and I have to go searching for those movies and shows.

So, people, hetero blinders off and look at the world around you. It is heterosexuals pushing their lifestyle onto us. We want the same freedom that you express every day.

Yes, people's sexuality is inherent. I grew up entirely around straight people, and it didn't make me straight. In fact, the fact that I didn't see anyone who was gay (and I clearly was attracted to the same not the opposite gender), that was an incredible point of confusion for me!

Nothing you do is going to make more or fewer gay people. The only difference is how we treat them once they realize who they are and how God created them.

And seriously, whether you are gay or straight, you are awesome exactly the way God created you. No one is promoting gay people over straight people. Geesh!

Michael Sam is the epitome of the American dream, and we should all be celebrating the fact that even a black gay man from rural Texas can work hard and become a professional football player. The fact that you use this moment to spew your ignorance is disgusting, and history will totally put you in the same bin as people who protest "race mixing".

Yep, the same people who kept black and whites from marrying. Same people who kept blacks from voting. Women from voting, all because of how they read the scriptures. Almost anyone who strongly opposed gays or marriages of are dealing with homosexuality themselves.

Opposing gay marriage is no different than when

people opposed marriage between races a few years ago. Opposing either one makes someone a bigot. The end.

Something I really hate is when someone who has no idea about what they are talking about tries to sound like some kind of authority on a subject they honestly know nothing about.

Oh, and from this point on, if anyone on any of my online profiles brings the subject up in any negative derogatory way, I will delete them without hesitation or warning. I do not debate this issue.

I seriously don't know of anyone keeping anyone on their Facebook friend list that is only there to say things to make them feel bad about who they are, so don't no one even think to convey that I am some kind of "bad guy" because I am speaking out about a certain matter that I am over on there.

I seriously am so over people *trolling* my friend list for a period of time so they can eventually make their stance on some particular subject known. I can't believe that people don't have more time and better things to do with their lives than that.

It plainly says in my profile information that I am interested in men, and I am in a relationship, so for the life of me I can't figure out why anyone who isn't intelligent enough to comprehend that either accepts or sends me a friend invite.

I really hate to remove anyone from my friend list on there, but I really don't feel like having anyone in my circle of friends who is going to speak up from time to time telling me they think I am wrong for being who I am. I just don't think that is healthy for either myself or the person doing it.

It's one thing to disagree on certain topics, like politics, religion, or entertainment, but I just don't see any reason to keep anyone around that is only there to tell me from time to time that they think I am wrong for being who I am.

Life is way too short, and I don't have time for such negativity in mine.

One of the many reasons I don't have time to tolerate some of the things I've mentioned on Facebook is because after not only a lot of people I loved passing away over the recent years, but after my own health scare a few years back (for those of you that don't know, a few years ago I had congestive heart failure, respiratory failure, a collapsed lung, and a blood clot in one lung, and was told I died for a few minutes and was revived) I have learned one valuable lesson: Life is *short*! We can all go at any moment, so don't waste time on anything that brings any kind of negativity into your life, only concentrate on the positive, and tell people what you think and how you feel about them every chance you get - you may not have another chance.

When I created some of my online profiles, I made sure to stay clear of any "issues", but after some recent posts I have seen, I want to make something perfectly clear:

I have long since lost count of the people I've

friended on Facebook that on the surface appeared to be open minded and kind hearted toward homosexuality, then the next thing I know their bigotry comes out in spades.

I think people get on there and troll profiles of people who are gay so they can "friend" them and then hit them with some kind of whammy later on.

I have actually had people troll my profile just so they could later let me know their stance on homosexuality. Trust me, I don't accept friend invites from just anyone, I only accept people I know, or mutual friends. It's usually people here in the same area I live that does this shit.

I am incredibly picky when it comes to establishing friendships with people. I can't begin to count the number of people that claim to have no problem at all with gays and then turn around and are the first ones to make sick jokes, criticizing us and disagreeing with every aspect of marriage and work equality.

When your ass can be fired in nearly half of the states in this county, simply based on who you are and who you love, then you can cry to me about sensitivity.

It's funny to me how people think that us gay people actually dream up all of the hatred, bigotry and stupidity we are faced with on a near daily basis. It's also funny how some think we make too big of a deal when we celebrate any of the accomplishments that occur in regard to gay rights/equality.

What would you like us to do? Sit quietly and never comment on this sort of stupidity? Just pretend we're all equal?

You know, I am sick and tired of some people saying that I don't like for someone to disagree with me, and then delete me the minute they see I have a different viewpoint than they do.

I mean, seriously, it's stated on my online profiles some of my "likes" and "dislikes", my political stance, my religious views, and my sexual orientation.

So, to me, when someone friends me and then turns around and does that, it makes them a troll. True story.

If you are some kind of small minded idiot who believes in your pea-sized brain that someone being homosexual is "wrong" or "sinful" or "against God", then please do yourself (and myself) a favor and click on the *delete* button now. You won't be missed, I promise you.

You know what I find disgusting? People who think it's disgusting for people to show affection for one another. What the fuck kind of world do we live in where violence and bloodshed is more acceptable than some forms of affection between two people? Seriously?!

It makes us no different/better than any other animal, hell, scratch that, than any insect on this planet! Piss ants have a better grasp of it than most humans!

I don't mind straight people as long as they act gay in public! Look, I don't mind if you're heterosexual, but you need to keep that mess in the bedroom.

I don't care what anyone does in the privacy of their own bedrooms. But I wish those hetero's would quit flaunting themselves about and having sex in public. They should go back in the closet so the rest of us aren't uncomfortable.

Heterosexuals and their "straight agenda" enough is enough!

Disgusting hetero's - why do they always have to push their lifestyle in front of everyone, including children. Why can't they keep their sexual preference private. I hope they don't try to get married or have kids. What is the world coming to!? Disgusting!

Gross. I wish they wouldn't flaunt it and shove it down my throat.

God made men and he made women, and these straights are going to put this country through hell if they insist on mixing the two. Stop trying to put chocolate in my peanut butter. I'm sick and tired of hearing heteros claiming to be born that way. No. You made a choice, just like I chose to be Gay! When I see heteros at the mall with their children, all I can think about is them having sex! Ugh!

In Genesis 1:28 it says "Be fruitful and multiply". This means to grow apples, pears, peaches and other various fruits, and when you are done with that go do your math home work. Heterosexuals have it all wrong, this has nothing to do with S - E - X and having children. The idea of having S - E - X is a made up idea from the Devil himself.

Dear Lord, I pray today for all the people who don't understand *satire* when they read it!

All gay people were created by straight people...why won't they stop making gay kids...maybe because it is not a choice....and is a natural human sexuality.....no matter how many times you see two guys making out or two women it is not going to "make you gay"...so your argument is mute.

I don't know how these idiots get on TV. It seems the stupider and less informed you are, the more likely you'll be a talk show host.

And, no offense, but if anyone thinks that some wormy little man like Joel Osteen is anywhere near being a "true man of God", then you need to buy a clue. True story.

I speak my own truth - anyone who still believes that being gay is a sin is a bigot, no different than those Christian bigots who still claim that race mixing is a sin. They should be ostracized from polite society. I still think it's important to call out bigotry, and bigots. Religious belief is no excuse for bigotry. It's not name calling to tell the truth.

The problem is people who are deeply insecure about their own sexuality and scared to death to admit it. So they use these religions to channel their own pathetic insecurities and hatreds. What they really hate is themselves - they hate their feelings, they are ashamed.

That's all it really is. Because the truth is, if you are secure in your own sexuality, you wouldn't care less what two consenting adults did.

II.

"Say what you will but I stand behind my beliefs."

Translation: I think what I think and form my opinion based on my limited exposure to gay people and my lack of understanding homosexuality. Whatever facts you may present mean nothing to me. Your personal stories and struggles will do nothing to erase the incorrect beliefs I possess regarding homosexuality. I was taught to believe in an invisible spirit. I will believe in that invisible spirit with blind faith. Facts and allowing the possibility that people are simply born different from one another I refuse to believe.

This is what's wrong with people of faith who close their minds and no longer practice love but unknowingly use religion and their beliefs as a tool of hate.

To all the people that say homosexuality is a choice… When did you choose to be straight? When did you sit down and make the conscious decision to be physically and mentally attracted to a person of the opposite sex? Do you remember actively making that choice about who you were going to be attracted to for the rest of your life? Did you *decide* to be attracted to your husband/wife/boyfriend/girlfriend?

No. You did not. And if you say you actively made that choice, you are lying.

Who you're attracted to is a chemical reaction that occurs with no choice or planning. Live and let live. It doesn't affect your life if people are gay. Grow up, move on and let people love whoever that are lucky enough to fall in love with. Nobody deserves judgement and discrimination for falling in love with a person of the same sex.

It is beyond ridiculous and an absolute atrocity that people still have an issue with who people fall in love with.

Also, just because you say your prayers and go to church doesn't mean you're a good person. Nor does abiding by a bunch of outdated rules in an oppressive book for fear of what will happen to you when you die. Try living decently and positively, without discriminating and judging every person that lives a little differently to you.

People, if you are so adamant about Christ doing away with all of the Old Laws, then why the hell are you still clinging to the "homosexuality is a sin" argument? Jesus Christ never uttered one word about homosexuality. Oh, wait, maybe He did in Matthew when He spoke about eunochs, saying how some were made that way by man, some were made that way by themselves, and some were *born that way*, and there are those (this is where you need to pay attention because He was referring to people like yourself) that do not understand.

See, that's the problem. You are speaking out about a subject you know *nothing* about. Are *you* gay? No? Then shut up! Until you actually know from experience what it feels like to be gay (or anything different than yourself), then you have no right to try to tell others they are wrong (or "sinful") for being that way.

You are ignorant and have no compassion for your fellow human beings. You are of the mindset that if it's wrong for you, then it must be wrong for everyone, and that way of thinking is what is wrong.

And, you people are going to have to stop participating with a *lot* of people if you don't participate in any kind of sinful lifestyle (by the way, someone being gay isn't a "lifestyle" anymore than it is a choice, it is a sexual orientation, and it isn't sinful).

If you know anyone who works on the Sabbath, you should stone them to death, and anyone who has had a divorce, well, throw stones at them as well, and disobedient children are to be put to death as well. And if your daughter is ever raped, make sure she marries her rapist, or put them both to death.

Oh, and you'll need to stop associating with anyone who eats seafood or plays/watches football (you know, that whole thing about the pigskin).

Those are things you should do if you're going to live by outdated and outlandish Bible codes.

12 verses against divorce. 4 against having sex with someone who is menstruating. 2305 about

money. 300 about social justice and the poor. And 24 about immigration but you all focus on the 7 about homosexuals? Ridiculous.

I just love how the right wing spread their tolerance and acceptance of others. Can't you just feel that great big ol' hug, wrapping around us? Oh, wait, that's their hands on our throats. Don't you just love how they want to throttle us with their love?

Oh, and how dare we fight back, because you know we'd be attacking their freedom. Yes, we're definitely the intolerant ones. It is very rude to point out bigotry. And very un-Christian and un-American of us as well.

There comes a point where denying someone basic rights over something they have no control of becomes an issue.

Imagine if you weren't allowed to go to school because you were a woman. You have no control over being a woman, but you deserve the education, don't you? Or take being African-American or Asian, and not being allowed to vote. They're American citizens but because they aren't white they wouldn't be allowed to vote, and they have no control of their race. Could you imagine living in a country like that?

That's what it's like for non-straight people every day. We have no control over our sexualities yet we are regarded as lower and denied rights we deserve. It doesn't matter if *you* disagree, by supporting denying humans basic rights, no matter what faith you believe in, it makes you a bad person.

When you talk about "biblical marriage" you are referring to 400 wives and 800 concubines, right? Or Lot getting drunk and having sex with his daughters because his wife is dead? The hypocrisy of these supposed "Christians" would be laughable if they weren't serious and flat out ignorant.

You can't pick and choose an abomination in Leviticus. If you argue religious freedom to discriminate against gay people but wouldn't discriminate against any other so called "sinners" it doesn't make you religious, it makes you a bigot.

My feelings about this come down to: No wars, no inquisitions, and no repressive laws have ever been instigated by the LGBTQ community. If Christians could say the same thing, I'd probably be less grumpy when they complain about intolerance.

True story for everyone to pay attention to: There is no, and I repeat NO "war" on Christianity! However, what there is a real *war* on is as follows: Gay people, poor people, black people, women, and anyone who isn't far right wing Republican.
And I declare it is time to fight back!

A scathing portrait of how insane the right wing have become...

LUNATIC FRINGE

I.

"The word Christian doesn't associate with God anymore, it associates with 'over pretentious assholes who believe they are better than everyone else ever'. Not to mention hate, homophobia, and close-minded. This is why everyone hates us." …

The Christian "right" has done more to turn people away from Jesus than Satan himself. Someone once told me that if Satan can't destroy the church he'll join it. Well, these "preachers" are proving that point. And they're making their followers twice the demons they are.

You know, it must be really sad to be a right wing conservative, because they hate pretty much anything they disagree with. They can't conceive of "live and let live" at all, and they waste all their time and energy trying to make everyone as miserable as they are.

I find it so interesting that people who want to throw the Bible in people's faces, when confronted with actual Scripture from the Bible letting them know they are wrong, they *still* try to cling to some idiotic argument instead of admitting they are wrong. It's sad, really.

And, honestly, I don't see that Christians are being persecuted. What I do see is people on the far right whining that they are being told to shut up when they say things that are obviously bigoted and/or prejudiced.

What I have seen, and do see now, are gay people, people of different races and nationalities, poor people, and any other "minority" being persecuted by the Republican right wing.

People are tired of that and wanting the world to move forward past all that negative behavior.

They pick and choose like all Christians as to what books and verses they will believe and apply to their life. This buffet Christianity is the norm. It is one of the reasons the stink over one verse in Leviticus on gays is so funny. We ignore almost all of Leviticus every day, yet when it fits our personal bigotry we clammer on about how important this one verse is. And that is the reason there are more than 33,000 different sects of Christianity.

Since the dawn of modern religion, Christianity has been nothing but a tool for governments to keep control of their citizens. It's a multi billion (maybe trillion) industry designed to keep people entertained and fearful of what might happen to them if they think too much or do things that somebody else says they're not supposed to do.

Phil Robertson is, unfortunately, the face of Christianity for many of us: a face of ignorance, hate, condescension and the unwillingness to think for oneself. It is a brainwashed face, a face with nothing real, meaningful or loving to offer the world. It is the face of Bible-rationalized bigotry. It is the face of a man who promotes pedophilia in the marrying off of 15-16 year-old girls. It is a face so proud in its ignorance, that it pretends to know more than scientists about the nature of the universe and the development of the human species. It is, furthermore, a face that would drag the rest of us back into the pit of fear, by postulating its God as nothing more than the sort of monster constructed to scare small children. I have no use for such a god as his.

So saying "blacks were happy" pre civil rights, that men should "marry and start teaching 15 year old girls" and compared homosexuality to murder and bestiality isn't bigoted or hateful and dangerous?

Never watched "Duck Dynsaty", and will not watch A&E. Plan to boycott any store that sells "Duck Dynasty" items. I choose not to support bigotry and hatred. Apparently, the almighty dollar caused A&E to have a change of heart. I think A&E made a BIG mistake.

God's Word doesn't call for anyone to be a bigot. True story.

I love how people immediately start throwing the "socialist" and "communist" remarks around when the Pope talks about social justice. It just shows me how far out of touch some Christians are with the message of their own religion.

You know, with so many TV stations that air nothing but Christian programming 24/7, and the atrocious Christian Mingle date site ads that run around the clock on pretty much every channel on television, and not to mention *lots* of other examples, could some *please* tell me how the heck is there a war on Christianity?!

I'll wait. Thank you.

It all boils down to this, Jesus Christ Himself never asked for or took one penny to go around helping people, spreading His Word, healing the sick, feeding the poor, etc. And He plainly said for people to give up all that they owned and follow Him. And that it would be easier for a camel to pass through the eye of a needle than a rich man to enter Heaven.

Most of these televangelists are nothing but snake oil salesmen who have a product and peddle it for the masses. Sad that so many are so gullible to buy into it.

Now, that's not to say that all churches, or that all television ministers are bad. My favorite example of a good one is Billy Graham Sr. He was a true man of God as far as I know. Too bad his son didn't take after him.

You know, I just love how these fundamentalists are so in your face about how they don't like this and don't like that, and don't agree with a lot of things you say or do, and don't agree with the way you live your life, and don't agree with most things you say or do, and the first time you politely reply, they start crying and call you the enemy!

Whether viewed as a historical figure, a religious figure, or a fictional character, one thing is certain: Jesus Christ was pretty clear about certain things that a lot of people who claim to be of His faith are clearly going against.

One was when He healed the sick, He didn't just heal those with jobs, and say, "All you motherfuckers laying on your couch back off."

When He fed the poor and hungry, He didn't declare, "Only those working step forward to eat, and all you bozos without jobs back off."

And when He said, "Love thy neighbor as thyself," He wasn't referring to only loving people with jobs, and hate on those that don't work.

Some people obviously need to buy a damn clue before they declare they are of the Christian faith. True story.

II.

"I think we risk becoming the best informed society that has ever died of ignorance."

America for some reason has become a nation of fools, where stupidity is allowed to run wild and free, where science is scorned and demonized, and those who use logic to the fullest are derisively called "intellectual snobs".

We have wasted so much precious time debating fools who think their scant knowledge on the subject trumps the findings of highly specialized scientists in their field. Our world is burning all around us and instead of putting out the flames we are locked in a dead-end struggle, having to butt heads with idiot deniers like you.

Sadly, Americans have become so apathetic and uninformed they can't be bothered to unplug their iPhone or turn off the Kardashians long enough to oppose anything, unless someone tries to reduce sugar in school lunches, of course.

It's really scary how dumbed down our society is becoming, and how people anymore praise ignorance, and get defensive and poke fun at people who show signs of intelligence.

Sometimes I feel there should be a minimum IQ requirement to post comments online, or speak in public.

We really need to stop making stupid people famous here in America. True story! Fox News is like *MAD* Magazine on Crack. It's a shame people don't see it for what it is. They should run a disclaimer: Not the real news, only a parody!

The media can communicate with Democrats by reading their thoughts, but Fox News has caught them because they can communicate without thinking at all. I try not to watch Fox - it's bad for my health I've decided.

I honestly don't know how any Christian can defend the stance of the modern day Republican party. The GOP is filled with vile, devious, conniving pricks who hate anyone outside their elitist ranks. Using semantics to cheat people is the least of their dirty tricks!

GOP business as usual. Hatred and Intolerance are at the very root of their core values.

Republicans bragging about their communication skills is like the cast of "Duck Dynasty" handing out grooming tips.

The Republican party has become rife with pure evil. They might want to actually meditate on the Word of which they are so fond. How does one determine if one's heart has hardened? Are you sensitive to the needs of the people around you? If you see a need, do you fill it or do you ignore it and/or start judging those in need?

What I really and truly don't understand is why

some people are trying to lay the blame on the poor people of this nation instead of looking at the uber-rich and saying, "Hey, you motherfuckers have way too much money, *you're* the problem with the economy!"

Everyone in this country (if not the world) should see the movie *American Psycho* to get a good idea of just what is wrong with this world today, and when and how it all kind of happened.

Especially one scene in particular between Patrick Bateman and a homeless man. It says all that needs to be said about the asinine mentality of the greedy Wall Street types that have popped up in the past few decades since the Reagan administration.

It literally sickens me when I hear some people say that poor people are poor because they don't work hard enough, or because they are lazy and want to take advantage of the government and want to live on handouts.

When in *reality* it's the people who have millions and billions of dollars hoarded in banks around the world that we should be more focused on talking about.

If aliens came to earth they'd think we were all retarded. People with more money than they could possibly spend in 1,000 lifetimes, and others with no food.

We fought a revolutionary war to end the power of kings in this country. Then we made new kings. I'm not against people being rich, and people who start a business deserve more than the people working for them, but not at this level of disparity.

You know, I think I am beginning to see what some Republicans meant when they said that most people are living above their means, though. It's not the poor, lower class that are doing it, but the middle class - the people who live in these mini-mansions, and install elevators in their house; they're the ones living far beyond their means.
Just a thought.

Something that kills me about the mentality of most people on the Right (and some on the Left as well) is the thinking that minimum wage shouldn't be raised because it will cause the cost of inflation to rise. Hey! Wake up! The cost of living has already reached staggering heights, and if the minimum wage isn't raised, then how the hell are people on low incomes supposed to survive?

And the other (and main) thing that makes me want to take an axe to some Conservatives (and some Liberals as well) is when they make remarks about how certain jobs are just temporary and not meant for people to retire on.

Hey! Here's a true story for all of you: Every job in this country matters! It doesn't matter if it's slinging burgers at a local McDonald's, or waiting tables at a local restaurant, working the cash register at a local food market, or digging shit out of toilets, *someone has to do those jobs*!

So, in that sense, it makes those jobs *important*

jobs! Understand?

And, by the way, not everybody is working a low-paying job until something "better" comes along. Do you know how many people with college degrees are working these low-paying jobs because there is nothing available in their field? Do you know just how many people are working these jobs because the job they had in their career field was reduced or moved to another country, and the company closed down and they have nowhere else to work?

It's time to make these damn millionaires and billionaires of the world come off a little of that money and start paying working people what they deserve! True story! And if you're opposed to that, then there is something seriously wrong with you! True story continued.

Ok, here's one of many reasons the uber-rich in this country need to stop being so greedy and start "sharing their wealth" by paying higher taxes and paying a higher minimum wage: Because one of the biggest rules of any business is that you have to sometimes spend money to make money. And if they continue to hoard their money while the middle class dwindles down to nothing and can no longer contribute to society, well, then they too will eventually dwindle down as well because there will be no one paying them for their products.

It's really that simple.

Here's how it works. When an employer pays his employees a living wage they have more money to spend. When they spend that money they create higher demand for goods and services. Higher demand for goods and services means that employers hire more people to meet that demand. More people working puts more money in the economy and the cycle expands.

The fallacy that Republicans try to shovel is that an $11 per hour wage will cause prices to go up in equal measure, but that's wrong because there are many more units sold than employees. For instance, McDonald's would only have to raise the price of a Big Mac meal by a few cents to make up the difference. In a consumer based economy like ours it's the consumer that created jobs, not the employer.

Here's a thought, instead of blaming the poor, and making remarks like, "Too many people are lazy and drawing money (and/or food stamps) from the government they don't deserve" why not focus on the *real* problem, and say things like, "No one needs to have billions of dollars!"

Why is it that someone has a room full of newspapers or magazines they are called a hoarder, but when someone has stacks of cash that have to be held in large vaults, they are put on the covers of magazines and worshipped? It makes no sense to me. Hoarding is hoarding, no matter what the actual thing is that someone is hoarding.

Seriously, why is it that when someone has a house full of magazines they've collected over the years, they are called "hoarders" and looked down on, but when people have so much money that they don't know what to do with it and have to open up several bank accounts to hold it all, they are put on the covers of magazines and worshipped?

I know this may not be a "popular" opinion, and frankly don't care, but I honestly don't think in this day and age that anyone should be allowed to have *billions* of dollars while the rest of the world goes hungry and/or are homeless. Nor do I think anyone should want to have that amount in these situations.

Times have got to change. Time to wage war on the spoiled greedy uber-rich. Just saying.

There is an increasing dependency on our basic needs. If we go into another depression or go to war, we will all starve to death!

It's the GOP that calls for less government for corporations while calling for more regulations on people, usually poor people. If you're poor and on food stamps, I would think that your children would be thrilled to get treats like the other kids. Or are people supposed to say to their kids, "We're poor, you can't have that."

All of us should eat healthier. The decision of what to eat is ours and not the government, let's keep it that way for everyone.

Notice that servants of corporations, banks, and stockholders -that is, the Republican party- are actually doing everything they can to make America a third world country: They want to get rid of labor unions, they don't want to help the uninsured get insurance, they don't want to provide the poor and the elderly with a basic standard of living. The Republicans want a class of Americans who are so desperate that they will take any job at any level of pay… just like the laborers in these third world countries.

People who complain that the reason people work at McDonald's and Wal-Mart is because they are unskilled and therefore should not complain about how much they make.

Remember when we used to do on the job training? When we used to train people how to do stuff instead of forcing them to go to an expensive vocational school, or worse, college to learn a skill? Want to learn how to weld? Get hired here and you'll be welding in three days. Forklift? One day.

But nowadays you have to have experience or know someone. There is absolutely no way an unskilled worker can become a skilled one without knowing someone or dropping more than 10 grand on school.

I'm a person who believes that people should be more tolerable of other people's views, and be of the mindset of "You think that way, and I think this way, and that's alright" instead of being so divisive, and insulting anyone with an opinion different than their own.

That's what's wrong with politics today, too many people not able to compromise anymore.

Reading through today's headlines, I think it's

high time that moderate Conservatives and moderate Liberals find their common ground and come together. The extremism (on both sides) is genuinely frightening. We need to regain our collective common sense.

The common sense people on both sides used to work together. The extremists have hijacked that process and have forgotten they were put there to compromise, not throw tantrums and shut down the government and make the President look bad. The people need to step up and vote out the obstructionists and corporatists.

Some deluded people think Americans are the only people in the world that have their freedoms. What absolute nonsense.

We've become such a divided nation so full of hate. Even under Bush it wasn't this bad. Now it seems people have no respect for others and the vile coming from them is truly disturbing.

You know, it is a *shame* that we have a decent intelligent President, who is trying his best to get things done for lower and middle class America, and there are just so many haters out there. I really don't get it.

We Democrats put up with your ignoramus redneck cowboy from Texas for *eight years* without a peep, so you can most definitely show the same respect in return when we have someone with half a brain in office.

I can still clearly remember like it was yesterday

how it was practically preached on a daily basis that if anyone showed any disrespect for President Bush then they were just unsaved un-American anti-Christian Communist scum who should leave the country. Yet, today those very same people who preached that now show President Obama the most blatant contempt and disrespect to the point of being outright disgusting and shameful.

(Well, the reason is because George W. Bush was chosen by God to rule over the people of God's favorite country. Therefore, we *had* to listen and obey because otherwise we would be punished by God!

Now, Obummer/NoBama? He's a Muslim Socialist, illegal alien, Commie, terrorist, demon from the bowels of Hell and we must defeat him so that God will once again shine His divine light and allow all of God's favorite flavor of people {vanilla} to live in peace and prosperity with strong, Christian, white men in charge, stay at home women in pearls cooking dinner, and minorities holed up in their little enclaves, only emerging for the purposes of washing our clothes, cleaning our homes, and maintaining our yards. Those are the good ole days the Conservatives pine for, right? Besides, it's all in the Bible, right next to the part where it explains how Jesus wrote the Constitution.)

Republicans are always trying to outlaw stuff they can't control their addiction to. Outlaw homosexuality then they won't be tempted by homosexuals. I remember Pat Robertson or one of these far right extremist holy rollers once said we are all tempted by the Devil's homosexuality, we all have to fight that temptation to be saved by Jesus.

Ummmm, no. We all don't fight our homosexual feelings, not that there's anything wrong with it, but sorry guy, not everyone is gay, just you and ten percent of all humans.

Republicans feel they need to legislate morality because they are themselves what they consider immoral and the only way they feel they can control their savage temptations is by eliminating them.

I get offended (and find it insulting) when a particular political party tries to take away rights from gays, women, the elderly, and are cutting food stamps and trying to defund healthcare so that they can not only starve people, but prevent them from having affordable healthcare. Yeah, that's very Christian, and not the act of a terrorist is it?

If Republicans put half as much energy into improving the country as they put into blocking legislation and being sore losers on elections, we would live in a much better country.

Oh my lord, what planet do some of these Republican people live on? I was watching "Face The Nation" a while back, and Eric Cantor said that President Obama selectively elected to enact "Obamacare". Seriously? Really? Huh?

Last I heard, it had been voted on and enacted as a *law* by the Supreme Court.

Maybe I was dreaming about that.

Somewhere in the basement of the U.S. Capitol, Republicans are wrestling naked in a jello pit to determine who succeeds Eric Cantor.

Funds for the Jello were possible thanks to the cuts made to the food stamp program. And John Boehner is drinking Jello shots.

Would that be with the ranking members of the Vehemently Heterosexual Committee?

The first rule of the Jello pit is to never talk about the Jello pit.

I find it highly ironic that there is a political meme being passed around on social networks with a quote from Tea Party Republican Ted Cruz, the guy who SHUT THE GOVERNMENT DOWN because he couldn't get his way, and has cost tax payers billions of dollars, accusing President Obama of abusing power.

Ted Cruz is such a miserable sorry excuse for a human being! And for him to show such blatant disrespect for such honorable and respectable men like John McCain and Bob Dole put him at the bottom of the gene pool in my eyes!

I hate to even remotely get "political", but I can't resist from talking about watching the State of the Union Address the other night, and the whole time the President spoke, all I heard was *common sense* over and over again, and then the Republicans spoke, and my ears wanted to bleed.

I seriously don't see how they can twist such

sensible things like raising the minimum wage, making sure women get equal pay, and creating more jobs into some "Liberal agenda"! I would hope to think that is an *American* agenda.

What I don't understand is that we heard from their own mouths, during the Presidential debates, Obama saying he is fighting for *everyone* in America -especially the lower and middle class, and Mitt Romney saying that 47% of Americans are low life moochers and he doesn't care about them, and isn't worried about the poor...AND PEOPLE STILL DECLARED THEY WERE VOTING FOR MITT ROMNEY!

Seriously, what the fuck is wrong with some people?

And another thing is that some of the people who are brainwashed into thinking that President Obama is some kind of anti-Christ Satanic Muslim who's going to take all of our souls to Hell, if you would pull your head out of Fox News for even a second, you may see that in *reality* what he is trying to get achieved is actually very "*Christian*"!

Yes, you may recall that Jesus Christ was about feeding the poor and healing the sick, and not just the ones who could afford it, the way the GOP is doing, you know what with cutting food stamps and trying to defund the Affordable Health Care Act, so that poor people not only starve to death, but also won't have proper health care.

You know, I just want to know, where were all the

people who are crying that Obama is taking away their freedom when Bush was in office and signed the Patriot Act into law, which practically stripped us of a *lot* of our freedoms? See, that's because I don't recall them ever saying a word then!

And, furthermore, what Obama is doing is no different than what Republican Reagan wanted to do with the Brady Bill back in the 80's. Yet again something I don't recall anyone saying anything about. Yet when Obama tries to get some kind of control on these damn assault weapons that *nobody* needs, people come out of the woodwork screaming.

The Republicans and Democrats switched sides about 50 years ago. Let's just say that any historical comparisons regarding racism are utter non-sense. Also, let's drop the crap about all presidents facing the same disrespect. Can you think of any other time in which a congressman yelled "you lie" during the State of the Union address? When Obama wanted to have a message for the American student (back in 2009), the protests were off the hook. There were actually threats against the local board of education (in NJ), and complaints from parents who did not want that "black man" speaking to their children. I can't believe you people who think that this is all normal. The list goes on and on and on, but you need to open your fucking eyes to see it.

By the way, it's not me who's been "drinking the Kool-aid", but all these people being suckered in by the Republican party, the Koch brother worshipping

Tea Party, and the Fox News crowd.

Do you want your faith represented by people who take food away from the hungry and then laugh about it? How about by people who think certain people deserve health care and others don't? The "Christian Right" is an oxymoron and it's embarrassing.

The Republican party has co-opted Christianity in the United States lock, stock and barrel. They use the red herring issues of abortion and gay marriage to hoodwink Christians into believing that God requires them to vote Republican. Meanwhile, they become more and more extreme. They throw the poor, the sick, and the defenseless under the bus every chance they get. They prop up warmongers, plutocrats and moguls. Their agenda is the *exact opposite* of what Jesus taught, and yet 79% of white Evangelicals vote Republican. What a sad state of affairs.

It also didn't help matters concerning Obama when right after his first victorious win, the Republican Congress held a secret meeting (which isn't so secret anymore since everyone knows about it) where they took an oath to vote against anything that the new President proposed, no matter if it was something they disagreed with or not. And *that* is what has kept Obama from being a 100% great President.

But of course all the people on the right who are glued to Faux News 24/7 can't handle facts, and all they focus on are bullshit talking points their own party brings forth.

You know, I really and truly don't understand the

mentality of the GOP at all! Even as much as I detest someone like Michelle Bachman or Sarah Palin, if I heard that either one of them were in the hospital recovering from a blood clot (or any other major health issue), I would be offering my condolences and wishing them well. I sure as hell wouldn't be making snide remarks, like GOP have been doing about Hillary Clinton when she fell ill a while back. Wow!

(I think a lot of people feel that the bigotry and hatred Sister Sarah Palin has spread while pretending to be all cute and hockey mom-ish has earned her a seat real close to the fire -- if you get my drift.)

Republicans are some of the most *hateful* people I've ever met. They *thrive* on tearing people down who don't look like them and believe what *they* believe. They claim to be *Christians*, but Jesus would *never* be a Republican.

That's what I don't like about a lot of people on the far right, sorry.
They have this selfish sense of entitlement, as if they think theirs is the only opinion that matters, and they're going to go out of their way to let everyone they disagree with know how wrong they are for thinking that way.

I don't mean to compare and despair, but has anyone ever noticed the extreme difference between two people who are Liberals disagreeing on something as opposed to two Conservatives?

Liberal example:

"Oh, I didn't know you thought that way. Cool, that gives me a different perspective to think about, thank you."

Conservative example:

"You're stupid for thinking that way, and un-American, you should leave this God fearing nation right now, you Liberal hippie scum."

And this is NOT exaggerated at all.

An Oklahoma Tea Party candidate has suggested stoning gay people to death. I fail to see how this will result in smaller government.

Just when you think those crazy Tea Baggers have hit rock bottom (no pun intended) they sink lower!

Maybe we should stone him to death??? Just so he knows how it feels? Also...BENGHAZI!!!

I betcha he picks up transvestite hookers after Sunday evening Bible study but only when he is on a crack binge because we all know you're not gay if they do it you.

So it *is* the Dark Ages. As Neil DeGrasse Tyson tells us, heading right back to the caves.

The Tea Party sure sounds like the Nazi Party of the 1930's

Now, had he suggested stoning politicians, I can see how that would work ...

He should move to Pakistan, they love that there.

He hopes to improve sales (of precision throwing stones) for the National Stones Throwers of American, who claim it is their right to throw stones, from the Old Testament!

Why are all the nut jobs out in force?

Every time I think that Republicans couldn't possibly get any lower, they lower the floor.

And, sorry folks. The economy will have to wait. No jobs bill for you. There's people having gay sex to obsess over and legislate.

Conservatives are constantly saying something either racist, bigoted, and/or offensive. Take your pick.

Please wake up! Thank you. Rant is now over. Go back to your regularly scheduled program, just don't turn back on Fox News.

III.

I have been watching Fox. It figures that when Obama frees a P.O.W., he turns out to be the worst P.O.W. in history!

Because that is what every POW dreams while coming home after being held hostage for 5 years: to be vilified by the Party that send him to the war.

Never thought I would see the day when bringing home a soldier was wrong. What has happened to us?

So is that how it works now, if you are a prisoner of war whose release is arranged by a Democratic Administration, you become a deserter unworthy of release? Yes that sounds like Faux "News".

You know what, if I was someone speaking out against the bringing home of an American soldier who had been a POW for several years, I would be *disgusted* with myself! True story!

I wouldn't care if they traded fucking *twenty* alleged terrorists to bring home an American boy, I would just be glad that the trade had been successful! Seriously, what the fuck is wrong with some people?!?!

Gotta love all the Republicans who cheered his release, before they remembered how they're supposed to hate everything.

Not everything. Only the President. Before this, they were hating him for not getting Bergdahl out of

Afghanistan.

You did hear about the black president didn't you? Yes, if it had been Dubya who got him released, the Fake News trolls would have been all over it and for it.

It all boils down to the same thing: the African American man with the funny name in the White House. Even when he does what they want to do, they hate him, and will extend that hatred to anything he touches.

What is chuckle worthy is when they promote their ideas for years, sometimes decades, and as soon as the President agrees they hate those same ideas.

Or they write a bill, and as soon as it's brought to a vote, vote against it.

Funny how the GOP "forgot" about Iran-Contra (1,500 missiles traded for U.S. hostages), or how Bush's crew allowed Bin Laden's relatives to leave the U.S. within days after 9/11.

You're expecting these people to remember beyond yesterday!! That's just unreasonable!

McCain, for one, can't remember what he said 3 months ago - on tape.

I guess all the shape shifting GOP forgets we can view the videos where they recant their original views and lie to us with a smile on their faces. Who can vote for these folks after seeing how they cannot be trusted to even state the truth about their own policies??

For those of you on the Republican side of the

fence who may not understand why I (and others) am so upset about your misguided and hypocritical "outrage" over the American POW being brought home, let me see if I can put it a way that you may better understand:

Where was the outrage from you all back in 2006 when some American soldiers raped and killed a Somali girl, and then killed her family and burned her body?

Oh, wait, that's right, there wasn't any!

And, even worse, when filmmaker Brian De Palma made his awesome anti-war masterpiece *Redacted* in 2007 depicting that action, everyone on the far right attacked him, calling him un-American for telling such a story.

Hell, one of your favorite people, Bill O'Reilly even went so far as to call De Palma the Devil for making the film, and called for a nationwide boycott of the movie, without ever seeing it.

Now, here we are just 7 years later, and someone who allegedly left his post and was captured and held for *five years* has finally been released, and you all are attacking him?

What the fuck is wrong with you people?!
Seriously?

No, I don't take the side of Republican or Democrat, I just take the side of Common Sense, sadly, something that has been sorely lacking on the Republican side for quite some time.

This is insanity running rampant. They're so eager

to sink their teeth into President Obama they don't care how unpatriotic, ignorant, or godless they sound. They're hell bent on destroying a soldier for political gain. It's the face of hate, and hate is both insane and ugly.

Obama could save a raft of babies from a school of nuclear powered Russian gay sharks while quoting Scripture and most white males will hate him for the publicity stunt it obviously was.

At this point if Obama rescues a puppy from a burning building the puppy will be accused of having rabies.

If he walked on water, Fox would complain that his feet got wet. And accuse him of not knowing how to swim. Or of waging a war against the boat making industry.

Or that he splashed somebody - and then they would use tax payer money to launch a multibillion dollar investigation and smear campaign.

If Obama walked on water, Fox and the GOP would blame him for the pollution that caused the water to be so thick it could be walked on, while hamstringing the EPA and voting to defund it.

Please, if Obama walked on water, some people would say that he was un-American because he couldn't swim.

If he laid a golden egg in the middle of every home in America, Bill O'Reilly would complain about it being too bright.

If Fox gives the Prez credit, the entire network will

disappear in a blue flame.

If Obama cured cancer, Fox News would accuse him of putting doctors out of work.

In fact, I am lactose intolerant and *that* is also Obama's fault!

It's raining today... What do you say, Obama?

I broke my leg and had to have surgery. Thanks a bunch, Obama!

I bumped my knee on my office desk last week. I know it was Obama's fault and plan to sue him.

And he started the Chicago Fire. Oh, wait, that was before he was born. No matter, Fox will say it anyway.

I'm just *know* he set the volcano off in Pompeii! EVIL THY NAME IS OBAMA!!

The San Andreas Fault is Obama's fault. they really should rename it to "Obama's fault".

What hypocrites!! If this was Bush they would have a ticker tape parade and say he is the best leader ever.

If Obama had *not* done the swap Fox would be saying that he didn't care about the missing American because he was White.

It's either Obama didn't care about America and left an American soldier there or Obama doesn't care about America because he negotiated with the enemy proving he is in league with the enemy and blah blah blah. Foaming at the mouth right wingers.

They're still pissed about Osama Bin Laden being dead.

They'll get there and somehow tie it in to Benghazi.

It's like a mad rant/mantra: Benghazi!! Berghdazi!! Benghazi!! Berghdazi!! Benghazi!! Berghdazi!! Benghazi!! Berghdazi!! Benghazi!! Berghdazi!! Benghazi!! Berghdazi!! Benghazi!! Berghdazi!! Benghazi!! Berghdazi!!

If you say Benghazi three times and click your heels, Sarah Palin will drop a house on you!

The same idiots who made Ollie North a hero for trading arms for hostages. Give me a break!

Actually I am waiting for the....wait for it! IMPEACH THE PRESIDENT! Just wait. They're working on it as we speak

They will take the high-road-for-slime and consider the POTUS weak.

The point is correct. Obama breathes, they complain. It is that bad.

Exchanging prisoners kills the POW economy. Thanks for killing more jobs Obama.

They need to have a ticker tape at the bottom of the screen that explains why this is way worse than sending arms to Iran in exchange for hostages.

Never mind that Obama was the reason this soldier was *rescued* in the first place. He traded *five* POWs from Gitmo for this soldier. Kudos to President Obama. I love him!

Sadly, Republicans will now use this to claim he is a part of the Taliban....and thousands of mind numbingly stupid people will call for his impeachment for it.

For those keeping score, Obama has had more success negotiating with the Taliban than with Republicans. Probably nicer to deal with.

That's because "we don't negotiate with terrorists"...and who fits the description of "terrorists" better than those who shut down our government!

I've never understood why people claim Obama shouldn't negotiate with terrorists. The same people say he should negotiate with Republicans. And the difference is ...?

Apparently, the Taliban is willing to compromise whereas Republicans are not. The Taliban aren't dedicated to the destruction of America like the GOP. The Republicans are the American Taliban.

I've voted for both Republican and Democratic Presidents. I will say this about our current President: he hasn't once invaded the wrong country; as Commander-in-Chief, his troops were able to find and eliminate the world's greatest terrorist; while President, the stock market has absolutely rocketed, and he has attempted to do something outlandish: give all Americans health care coverage. Anyway...

Whatever Obama does is wrong. There isn't anything else to discuss. If he negotiates he's weak. If he doesn't he's stubborn and inflexible.

Initial reports are that after President Obama pee'd this morning, he left the toilet seat up. Republicans are outraged and want a formal congressional investigation.

The GOP went Full Racist Monte at the outset of Obama's presidency, and there's no erasing that gross picture because it's baked in.

I can't believe Obama is still in office after he killed bin Laden *and* got a POW home alive. That rat.

The Republicans' negativity is really getting old. I just don't understand why people still vote for them. They accomplish absolutely nothing.

Reagan taught us the proper way to trade for hostages is to give the terrorists advanced weaponry and Bibles.

But to keep them hostages until it makes the other guy look weak so you can steal the white house

Republicons had no problem sending him to war only a problem with bringing him home.

What really pisses me off is that the vast majority of people criticizing the release have never served in the armed forces or spent a minute in a war zone. Imagine the tune they would be singing if their asses had been captured for 5 years. These are despicable human beings.

If Bush had gotten bin laden, Republicans in congress would be calling for him to be added to Mt Rushmore.

75% of Fox viewers say Obama should have done more to prevent 9/11.

All his fault. Shoulda never given him the keys to the time machine!

GOP answer for not taking care of the veterans: send them back to Iraq!

Talk about hypocrisy taken to a sickening level, just look at how those on the far right are speaking out against Bowe Berghdazi's dad having a beard, saying it makes him look like a terrorist, yet in the same breath they pretty much idolize and worship some piece of shit right wing backward ass backwoods ignorant bigoted/prejudiced cretins like the guys (if they can be called such) from "Duck Dynasty".

Give me a fucking break!

The Taliban are not terrorists. They never attacked us. The only reason they were fighting Americans is because we went there and removed them from power.

As he has done several times in the past, it looks as though the President is playing chess while his detractors are barely playing Chutes And Ladders. All five of these guys we traded for Bergdahl would have to be returned anyway at the end of the war according to the international rules of war. The end of this war will be reality by the end of this year.

So we didn't necessarily set them free in exchange for Bergdahl, as much as we merely granted them a six month early release. And they weren't turned over to the Taliban, they were turned over to the Afghan government. If they are the dastardly evil doers the people on Fox want you to believe, it's up to the Afghan government to prosecute them, not us.

Exactly like how we handed over SS officers after WWII to be prosecuted at Nuremberg.

Bergdahl's status as a deserter, even if he is in actuality just that (which has yet to be proven, let alone litigated), is secondary to his status as an American soldier, who we do not leave behind. As always with this president though, it's not about the event, it's about how they can spin it to try (unsuccessfully) to hurt him.

Sometimes negotiating works well in the end. Republicans could learn from this.

I just want to clarify that my bashing of the Republican party in no way is meant to offend and/or insult any of my friends and/or family that are Republican. I appreciate and respect each and every person in my life, and respect different political (and religious) views than my own.

I just don't care too much for the clown car that is in political office these days, that's all.

We need to get every single rational Independent and Democrat to really look at what has happened over the course of the last six years and get to the most important election cycle in U.S. history and vote the bastards out. We can't wait two more years to see Democrats swept into office after more GOP obstruction and muck raking and scandal creation has driven our economy back into the recession they created in the first place. So my question is will *we the people* do the right thing.

It's time for everyone to stop worrying about party

and start voting for what is best for our country. The divisiveness of the current political climate makes it impossible for our Congress to get anything done. It is destroying us.

You know, I am constantly seeing things that I feel are attacking me for the way I live coming from the Conservative Right.

Like I said before, it is time to FIGHT!

A stunning non-fiction excursion into politics and religion, child-rearing and rules of grammar that will shock the senses...

THE FINAL DIATRIBE

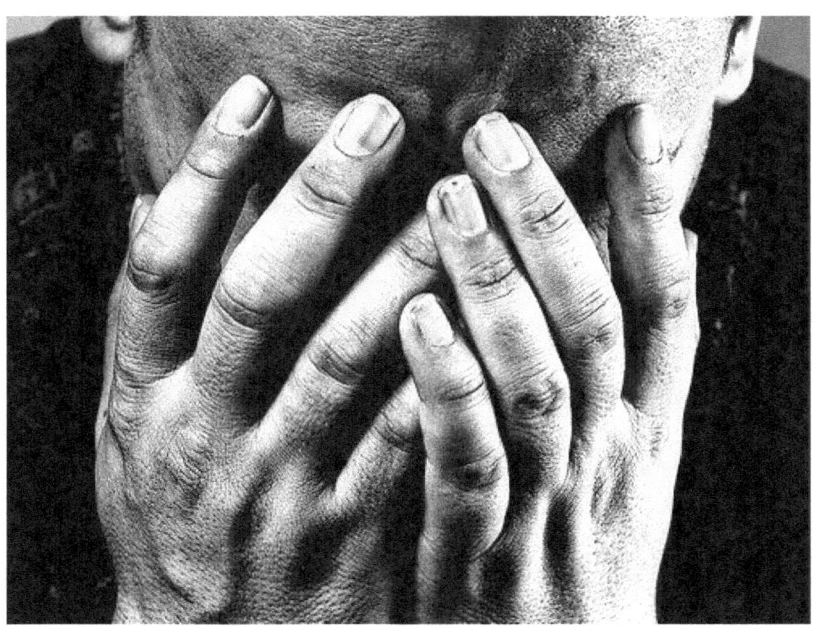

E.
"Political Rant…"

I am not a political person, and have even apologized in case I've offended people who are Republican/Conservative with links and posts I share on my Facebook page, because it is stuff claiming they are racist, homophobic, close minded bigots. Well, again, sorry if that stuff upsets you, especially if you're not a racist, homophobic close minded bigot, but that is all I am seeing and/or hearing from the Republican camps these days, so I am going to share stuff like that to help warn people away from them.

And if that offends anyone that is Republican/Conservative, then maybe it's time you ask yourself why it offends you.

Because it offends the hell out of me to hear some brain dead morons like Rick Santorum, Sarah Palin, Michelle Bachman, and several others in the Republican Party make idiotic homophobic, racist, bigoted remarks like they do.

So, maybe it's time you all look inside your own political party and be offended by them instead of trying to defend their sorry ass and claim you're offended by someone like me for simply sharing what they said!

Now, as some of you more than likely know, not all people that are Republicans are immature, narrow minded bigots. Some are really good people, and not only that, but are open minded and open to criticism of their political party.

But then there are those that are like whiny children, that if you say anything that goes against their way of thinking, well, boo on you, and you're gonna hear how offended and/or upset they are.

My "political" leanings are that of a moderate and I stay right in the middle where the world makes sense in the beautiful color of grey. Being in either party is an outdated concept at this point. Both parties have let this country down on so many levels. I refuse to agree with someone like Bush, Kerry, Gore, or McCain just because I belong to the same party. I listen to what the candidates say and what they have done, I don't give a crap about what party they belong to. That, and I try to avoid candidates who are overly religious and seem to think we were founded as a Christian nation, and infuses Christian values into his domestic or foreign policy. There are some great quotes from our founding fathers that state what they truly think about religion. You would be shocked....but that's neither here nor there.

You know, if I was part of a political party (or religion) that started promoting things like homophobia, racism, anti-women's rights, etc etc, I would leave that party (or religion) so quick it would make their heads spin. I don't understand why others can't do the same. If you're part of something that you don't believe in 100%, then why be part of it? And if you remain, then it signifies that you *do* support those beliefs even though you may disagree. Just something to think about.

Sorry, but it has boiled down to the fact that there is too much hate, prejudice, and negativity coming from the Republican camp, and even though you may not feel the way they do, if you support the party you are by proxy supporting the candidates, and obviously are against pretty much everything I stand for.

What moderate Republicans need to realize is that their party has been taken over by a bunch of right wing religious bigots, being the Tea Party people. Anyone who has watched the debates and observed the people in the audience not to mention the mean hateful remarks by all of the candidates. That coupled with being in bed with the 1%. No one but the rich or the bigoted should be voting for any of these candidates.

What really irks the hell out of me about the whole Right Wing mentality is that they have the mindset of an ignorant uneducated spoiled child who thinks that if it feels wrong for them, then it must be wrong for everybody. They can't seem to get it in their head that other people think differently than them, and have the right to do so.

I love people that get politically educated, and can admit their party has been completely shameful for the last 30 years! This is happening a lot out there, people. People are finding out the truth. It's the awakening. Get informed with facts, and you could be one of them. If more lifetime Republicans would pay attention to what the "new" GOP is up to, they would be holding up the same sign! Too many of them don't bother and just hide their heads in the sand because they don't want to deal with reality.

In all my years I have never been a "political" person, but upon seeing, reading, and hearing all the ignorant, hate-filled, homophobic rhetoric that keeps coming out of the Republican Party's camp, is it any fucking wonder I *hate* Republicans, and can't for the life of me understand how anyone in their right mind would ever want to be associated with such a fucked up bunch of retards!

I am sick and tired of all this bullshit that the Republicans keep wasting our time, energy, and good hard earned tax-payers' dollars on.
Sorry if this offends anyone, but if it does, so be it.

People should know that the entire Republican Conservative Right Wing mantra of "I've got mine, you get your own, we help those who help themselves, survival of the fittest" is the farthest thing from the Christian "rule" that they allege, and is taken straight out of Anton Zandor Lavey's *The Satanic Bible*.

If you don't believe me, then do yourself a favor and *read it* sometime!

I just want to set the record straight on something:

I have known several people that are Republican and are some of the finest, brightest, kindest people you'd ever hope to know, so I mean no offense to them. But this new crop of bat-shit crazies are giving everyone in the Republican Party a very *bad* name!

And to defend and/or support them just because they are Republican is just *insane*!
Remember that time when we elected that Republican President and he balanced the budget, reduced the size of government, and got us out of debt?

Yeah, me neither. Just saying.

It's really simple: With no middle class, society will crumble. Who do you think carries the lower class, and supports the upper class? Yep, the middle class! And these politicians bent on continuing to rob the middle class and drive them out of existence needs to be voted out of existence. That simple.

We are quickly becoming what our enemies love, and as we seemingly begin to tear our country apart through divisive politics, character assassination, bigotry, hatred, mistrust, and false innuendos, our daily news has become comic fodder for the enemies of the United States of America. To the World, we have become the Divided States of America. If we are to be The Greatest Nation on Earth -The Pinnacle of Civilization- then it's time we start acting like it!

"Patriotism is not short, frenzied outbursts of emotion, but the tranquil and steady dedication of a lifetime."

"It's not the volume of your argument that will change an opponent's mind, but rather it is the value of your argument that will ultimately win the day!"

I just want to say that even though I make a lot of anti-Republican remarks, my "fight" isn't against either political party. No, what I am taking a stand against, is that in this day and age there is *no* place for ignorance, intolerance, and bigotry from *anyone*, be they Republican or Democrat. I am literally sick and fucking tired of seeing and/or hearing people in such positions of power making such immature, ignoramous, idiotic, hateful, harmful, homophobic remarks. I found it repugnant when I was seeing some people trying to compare our current President to Adolph Hitler, but in the meantime all the real modern day Adolph Hitlers are out and about spreading their bullshit without any retribution at all.

It is time for this to STOP!

I, myself, can easily pick up a Bible and take anything in it to suit an "agenda", and say that it applies to what I want it to, just like everyone else can do; and so many are currently doing. Again, it is time for this bullshit to STOP!

We are not living in the Dark Ages, but if this shit continues, we soon will be. Think about it! Thank you!

As I've said time and time again, I am not a "political" person. And I know over the past few months I have been kind of slamming the Republican party. And, trust me, when I see and/or hear the

Democrat party making as many horrendously stupid mistakes, I will make mention of that too. But so far, I have only seen the GOP being the goofballs!

I respect everyone's political party choices. However, when I see and hear with my own eyes and ears some of the bullshit coming out of the mouths of some of the up-and-coming GOP party candidates, all I can say is PULL YOUR HEAD OUT OF YOUR ASS, PEOPLE!

No one should have the right to tell someone else who they should or should not love! That's not what politics are supposed to be about! It's time to stop the bullshit!

And you know, since I'm not really a political person, it is only recently occurring to me that since 1980 we've only had *one* Democrat President, and that was the *only* time we weren't at war with anyone, and the economy wasn't only "fixed", but we were in the surplus!

Look back and it's obvious that Reagan and Bush Sr. wrecked the economy, and then Clinton came in and straightened out everything and got us ahead financially, and then Bush Jr. came along and wrecked the country almost beyond repair.

And now that the first Democrat to be in office since the 1990's isn't fixing things fast enough, people are ready to toss him out and put in another Republican.

Oh dear God, give me a fucking break! Get real, people! This country can't and won't survive another

Republican administration.

You know, it's a sad testament to the right wing's mentality that when you look back on the Clinton administration and realize that the first Democrat president we had in over 10 years - someone who did an awesome job getting this country back on track economically- and the right wing Republicans spent millions of tax payers' money to try to find some kind of corruption so they could boot him out of office.

And, lo and behold, Kenneth Starr finally succeeded in having him impeached over receiving a blow job!

And, now here it is a little over 10 years later, and the first Democrat to be in office since then, you are pouncing on and attacking, trying your damndest to drive get him out of office.

You know, Clinton may have slept around some while he was in office, but frankly I don't care what people do in their private lives. He got our country out of debt and into a financial surplus. And then Bush came along and started *two* unfunded wars and put us right back in a huge debt. Sure, Obama has had to spend some money to try to fix the deficit, but haven't you ever heard the phrase: Sometimes you have to spend money to make money.

Plus, he has a Republican congress fighting him every step of the way right now. If you voted any Republican in office at this point, you could say goodbye to programs like Social Security, SSI, Medicare, etc, because they are wanting to do away with them. Obama is fighting to save them.

And what's really hurting our nation right now is all the jobs being sent over sea's, and tax breaks for millionaires. Republicans did that, not Democrats.

When Bush was in office, he started with a balanced budget and a surplus. Wages declined, as well as jobs. 9 points of the GDP had declined. He waged two wars, one needlessly. In 2007 the housing industry crashed, just weeks before Obama stepped into office. In 2009 the stock market crashed, GM and Chrysler went bankrupt. The Wall Street corporate welfare bailout that cost us 60 billion dollars last year alone (yes we are still paying for it), not counting the expensive "cowboy approach" to foreign policy, and we were losing 750,000 jobs a month! So Repubs, you left us a total mess and we are not cleaning it up fast enough? Thanks but no thanks, you have helped us enough. And like a child throwing a temper tantrum you obstruct progress because you didn't get your way.

Wow, please tell me all you Republicans just how proud you are of your political party!

If you're for this modern Republican party, then you're for pretty much against everything I stand for, and don't really see why we should be friends any longer. Sorry, but the truth is the truth. Republicans represents everything I am against (greed, homophobia, anti-women), and anyone who supports them supports those agendas, and I really wouldn't want to be friends with someone who would support that.

What I see going so wrong in politics today is that "fiscal conservatives" (which is a good thing, believe it or not) have been taken over by "social conservatives" (which is a very bad thing), and instead of trying to "fix the economy", we now have a bunch of idiotic people trying to "fix society". And it's not society that needs fixing! Fix the economy, and society will fix itself!

And sorry, but I take it as a personal afront if anyone that I consider a friend votes for Republicans. I am an openly gay man, and anyone who supports the Republicans' outdated homophobic mentality is pretty much saying they are against my way of living, and I don't see why we should be friends. Sorry if you can't understand that!

I just love how conservative Right Wing nuts can't grasp why people were boycotting Chik-Fil-A because of the restaurant supporting Hate groups, but yet they want to boycott a small owned pizza business because the owner hugged the President! Wow! Talk about your fucked up priorities! Wow!

Imagine if someone spent eight days trashing their house and then hiring you to clean it up, the whole time their kids kept running around and interfering and slowing you down, and then you are told you didn't get it cleaned in time, and then proceeded to blame you for the mess it was in.

Now, take that and apply it to the Obama administration. Same thing.

You know, seriously, I would feel like the biggest piece of shit that ever walked this planet if I was a wealthy person (with an income of over a million dollars), and instead of doing what I could to help others (example: paying more in taxes), I spent millions of dollars trying to buy Republican politicians to help me not pay higher taxes! What the fuck is wrong with some people?!

Yes, ladies and gentlemen, the Republicans are STILL WANTING TO LOWER TAX RATES FOR MILLIONAIRES AND RAISE TAXES ON THE MIDDLE CLASS! Does this make sense to you?!

"Republicans care nothing for the disabled, the poor, the middle class, no one! They exploit religion to get votes from the religious right and exploit issues of abortion, gay marriage, and women's rights. They claim to be Christian but they're not. They only care for the ultra rich. Going against everything Jesus preached. Hypocrites! These people are just horrible excuses for the use of flesh!"

The GOP has become the party of intolerance to any beliefs but their own even if they are majority views. The GOP's attitudes to women, poor, minorities, LGBT are all extreme on the nasty end, and if *you* vote for this, you are advocating for it and giving your stamp of approval. So before you pontificate about the goodness of your party, step back and educate yourself on the values your party espouses.

It is time for the GOP to go the way of the wigs,

and simply disappear. They are no longer relevant, like VHS, or Tube television. Not a single Republican today understands the modern world we live in; it is only going to get worse for them.

There is world hunger to worry about, two unfunded wars still going on, a huge unemployment problem, and people want to argue over who can marry each other. Give me a fucking break!

Do any of these Right Wing idiots ever stop and think that when they say shit like, "Well, being gay is a choice, people choose to be gay", that it's not only an insult to homosexuals, but it's also really a huge slap in the face of heterosexuals everywhere?

Think about it: It's like they're saying, well, being gay is a choice, so that means you choose to be gay, so in essence, *no one* is really heterosexual either, because at any given minute you could decide to be gay for a while. Just saying.

Pretty much *all* conservative politics are selfish at their core. Take any conservative position on a social or economic issue and boil away all the rhetoric and what you are left with is "I got mine, screw you".

A list of conservative ideas and what they really mean:

1. No gay marriage – Homosexuality makes me uncomfortable (due to misguided religious influence or poor upbringing or both) so gay people should be punished because of my beliefs. Stoopid homos…

2. No welfare, food stamps or Medicaid – I'm not poor enough to qualify for these programs so my tax dollars shouldn't pay for it. Stoopid poor people and by poor I really mean black...

3. No health care reform – Why should I help pay for other people who are sick when I'm not? Stoopid sick people...

4. No environmental protection – Environmental laws makes things more expensive for me and that's bad. I also don't understand the concept of long term impact; I want cheap gas and gadgets now! Stoopid...ah, you get the idea...

5. Don't raise my taxes – *ever*. The government can find its own money to pay for stuff I want.

6. Medicare – Young conservatives: Why should I help pay for old people and the disabled? Older conservatives: Keep your government hands off my Medicare!

7. Social Security – Young conservatives: Sacrifices need to be made, people should take care of themselves, not depend on handouts from people like me. Older conservatives: Sacrifices need to be made BUT DON'T YOU

TOUCH MY SOCIAL SECURITY!
8. No abortion – The government should tell women what to do with their bodies because I don't like abortion.
9. No prayer in school? – GOVERNMENT OVERREACH! I like The Jesus™ so everyone should have to listen to my prayers. No Muslim prayers, though. That's indoctrination.

The real disgrace in America isn't the cowardly and appalling behavior of the Right Wing liars and propaganda pushers who constantly poison media airwaves with ideological hate speech and ugly political rhetoric.

Nor is it the inability of GOP congressional members to pass legislation designed to help lift the American people out of the depths of the worst economic disaster to face the country in 80 years.

The real shame in this country is the fact that so many gullible and narrow-minded people are eagerly willing to accept the fear inspired ignorance, the racist tinged stupidity, and the abysmal political hypocrisy that is found in the modern Republican Party.

The country stands at a pivotal time in history. Our nation can remain a shining beacon of light which attracts people from all over the world – looking for a better way of life. Or, we can continue to embarrass ourselves by blindly following the extreme elements of American society into the most ugly and despicable recesses of human existence.

Our choices are clear: We can plot our own course of political action by joining hands in an all-out effort to create jobs, repair our crumbling national infrastructure, and care for our elderly, the poor, and the sick - or we can allow the Right Wing "Gilligans" to steer the ship of state into a socio-economic wasteland, with no contingency plans and no hope of rescue.

I find it amusing how GOP supporters keep calling for impeachment whenever there is a Democrat in the White House. I don't recall any outrage when one of their own purposely lied to the American public to start an unwarranted war, cost the lives of so many American troops and destroyed our economy. Where were the calls for impeachment then? Instead, the American people thought it "wise" to re-elect.

You know, I don't understand all the hate for the President. It doesn't matter what someone's political party is, they should still respect the standing President in office. Even though I couldn't stand George Bush, I still respected him as our President when he was in office.

And, what happened to "Respect your President"? Especially during war time! Remember when the Dixie Chicks calmly spoke out, simply saying they were embarrassed that the President was from Texas, the same state they were from? And people everywhere wanted to burn them alive! Wanted to kick them out of the country!

Yet, now that there is a Democrat (and a black man at that), it's like it's a whole new ballgame, and people everywhere are speaking out belligerently, expressing their disrespect for him.

Seriously, what happened between then and now? What changed?

Not sure anything changed. It's just the way one group behaves compared to another group. For example, when liberals don't like a President, we make fun of him and laugh. When conservatives don't like a President, they spew vile, insane, foaming at the mouth, hatred.

Top Ten Reasons It Sucks To Be A Republican:

I can only imagine how difficult it would be to try to do just some of the following:

1. Find a biblical reference to justify hate or greed or selfishness.
2. Convince women that the government should be in control of their reproductive choices, not their doctors or, heaven forbid, themselves.
3. Explain why fracking and fracked water is good, while solar and wind power (and even vegetable gardening) are simply a plot to take over the world.
4. Explain why you should absolutely have to have an ID to vote, and why you should absolutely not have to have an ID to purchase an assault weapon.
5. Justify your agenda of arming every man, woman and child as your Christian duty, when Jesus said "Put down your weapons."
6. Convince minorities that they need to join the same political party as the KKK, the Aryan Nation and the Teabaggers carrying signs that say "There's a Muslim, Kenyan, Socialist N*gger in the White House." (Generally

spelled incorrectly, but still…)

7. Pretend that Fox News is a source and use it to defend your arguments when discussing the war on Christmas and the Easter bunny.
8. Explain for the 47th time why trying to repeal healthcare is not a waste of taxpayer resources.
9. Justify gutting workers' rights and fair wage policies by claiming those policies are "bad" for workers.
10. Convince the masses that government is not trustworthy, while at the same time removing policies put in place to help keep the government trustworthy.

The biggest problem in our country is that we've allowed the elite to destroy our public education system. Many public schools around the country, especially in major metropolitan areas, look like clown school and gladiator school are sharing space in the same building.

As the leadership of any dictatorship will tell you, controlling the masses is a simple matter of keeping them stupid and afraid. Do that, and they become as pliable as soft clay.

Can you feel the potter's wheel spinning?

II.

"Christianity Vs. Homosexuality…"

I don't normally talk religion, but I just want to say that I believe that when you take everything in the Bible and condense it to its basic core message, it's such a simple message:

Love other people. Help other people. No matter who they are, or what they do. Forgive other people. That simple. So sad that so many people can't seem to grasp this.

I honestly don't know which one is worse: People who believe in a bunch of superstitious mumbo jumbo, or the religious and political leaders who prey on those who do. Why worry about how other people have sex or what obscure Bible passages really mean when you can barely make your house payment each month?

This isn't what Jesus was about. What did he say? "Love one another as I have loved you" and "Don't judge." How easy is that? The greatest Commandment is "LOVE ONE ANOTHER"- why have we not learned that by now?!

If you're going to claim that you stand up for Biblical principles, stand up for them...but that means stand up for all of them. Don't just stand up for the ones that give you a person to hate or an innocent victim to attack. Stop wearing polyester, and stop watching football, and go marry your dead brother's wife.

I have no problem with people standing up for their religion, but I do have a big problem with people standing up for hate and trying to say it's because of religion.

Something I've always got a kick out of hearing all my life is straight people saying, "I don't have a problem with gay people, I just wish they wouldn't shove it down everyone's throats."

Well, when you grow up gay with everything around you (movies, books, songs, etc etc) shoving heterosexuality down your throat, it really only seems fair to be able to talk about homosexuality as openly as everything else. Seriously, what's the problem?

Ok, I've given it some thought today after getting a message from someone this morning informing me that she was a Christian and believed that the Bible says it is a sin for anyone to be homosexual, and I've decided that since people want to believe that bullshit, then here's a few more rules from there that we need to abide by:

1) Women should be treated as 2nd class citizens.
2) Get a divorce and get stoned to death! No exceptions!
3) All disobedient children must be put to death. No favoritism shown here

either!

4) If you get raped then you must marry
    your rapist or be branded a sinner!
5) Everyone should own at least 2 slaves!
6) No eating pork or you'll burn in Hell!
    No lie!

Oh yeah, and men are allowed to have as many wives and/or concubines that he so pleases! Amen!

And that's all for now, but I am sure there are others I'm not remembering at the moment.

And if you think I'm making this shit up and don't believe that it's in the Bible, well you should check it out for yourself because it is all in there!

FUN FACTS ABOUT THE BIBLE AND HOMOSEXUALITY:

(I've saved this list for use in response to right-wing bigots who often condemn homosexuality by misusing the Bible in order to support their own hatred. Here it is...)

1.) Leviticus is an ancient Jewish cleanliness code, and does not apply To Christians. It only applies to observant, orthodox Jews. It also bans shellfish, football on Saturdays, sleeping with a woman who's on her period, and mixing fabrics.

2.) Sodom was destroyed for inhospitality and its mal-treatment of the poor. Not because of homosexuality. The crime in Sodom was attempted rape -- not homosexuality.

3.) The Ten Commandments say *nothing* about homosexuality.

4.) Jesus says *nothing* about homosexuality.

5.) *No part* of the Bible mentions homosexuality *as we know it today*!

6.) Paul, in writing to the Romans, was upset because people were using Temples for orgies -- *not* because of the *type* of orgies or the *type* of sex which was occurring.

7.) Even Christians believe that sex is for more than just procreation. It is a *human* way of expressing love, affection, and desire.

8.) The word "homosexuality" did *not* even exist at the time the Bible was written.

9.) The current-day versions of the Bible *cannot* be taken literally because there are *so* many versions and *so* many interpretations of it. The Bible must be *interpreted* and read, prayerfully and thoughtfully ... *not* literally.

10.) In short, the Bible and Jesus do *not* condemn the loving act of homosexuality, when it occurs in a non-exploitive way, between two consenting adults, who are not related by blood.

11.) GRAB A CLUE!

The Bible is a book about God — not a book about human sexuality.

The Bible is the story of God's love for the world and the people of the world. It tells the history of God's love at work rescuing, renewing, and empowering humankind. It was never intended to be a book about human sexuality.

In fact, the Bible accepts sexual practices that we condemn and condemns sexual practices that we accept. Lots of them! Here are a few examples:

DEUTERONOMY 22:13-21
If it is discovered that a bride is not a virgin, the Bible demands that she be executed by stoning immediately.
DEUTERONOMY 22:22
If a married person has sex with someone else's husband or wife, the Bible commands that both adulterers be stoned to death.
MARK 10:1-12
Divorce is strictly forbidden in both Testaments, as is remarriage of anyone who has been divorced.
LEVITICUS 18:19
The Bible forbids a married couple from having sexual intercourse during a woman's period. If they disobey, both shall be executed.
MARK 12:18-27

If a man dies childless, his widow is
ordered by biblical law to have
intercourse with each of his brothers in
turn until she bears her deceased husband
a male heir.
DEUTERONOMY 25:11-12
If a man gets into a fight with another
man and his wife seeks to rescue her
husband by grabbing the enemy's
genitals, her hand shall be cut off and no
pity shall be shown her.

I'm certain you don't agree with these teachings
from the Bible about sex. And you shouldn't. The list
goes on: The Bible says clearly that sex with a
prostitute is acceptable for the husband but not for
the wife. Polygamy (more than one wife) is
acceptable, as is a king's having many concubines.
(Solomon, the wisest king of all, had 1,000
concubines.)

Slavery and sex with slaves, marriage of girls aged
11-13, and treatment of women as property are all
accepted practices in the Scriptures. On the other
hand, there are strict prohibitions against interracial
marriage, birth control, discussing or even naming a
sexual organ, and seeing one's parents nude.

It kills me that so many people who believe in a
religion without even knowing what the religion
entails. Way too many people declare "I believe in
Jesus because the Bible tells me so", yet have no real

knowledge of what's actually said in the Bible. Word up: If you're going to follow something, find out everything you can about it before you invest yourself into it.

(And, this isn't a slam on any religion, just a remark about how some people who falsely claim to be something they don't have a real clue about.)

It is wearing me out how these fundamentalists are wanting to quote Scripture when it comes to homosexuality, but they ignore all the other shit that is now so outdated that even God ignores it!

I think I'm just going to start quoting Aesop's Fables from now on as a guideline to live by since so many other people are quoting another book of parables to live by.

You know, several years ago I came to the conclusion that the whole "Sodom and Gomorrah" story was probably one of my favorite stories in the Bible, because I love the whole parable about not looking back on bad things in life because it will freeze you like a pillar of salt. Great message! Too bad too many people want to try to get some kind of "God hates homosexuals" message out of that!

Real Christians look for the good in people, and try to encourage and help others out, not sit around and look for the bad in people and judge them, and think they're better than everyone else.

I love to be-friend people who I can agree to disagree with, and anyone who knows me will attest that I am one of the most tolerant people they know, but one thing I do *not* tolerate is people who want to shove their opinions down people's throats and try to bully them into believing the way they do.

I'm not one to bash anyone's religion, for I believe that is something that is personal to each and everyone's beliefs. However, I do question any religion that treats anyone as second class citizens, whether it is someone of a different faith, someone of a different race, gender, or sexual orientation. My belief is that if any religion tells me that someone is "wrong" and "beneath my way of thinking", then I believe that is a cult, for only a cult would want to try to divide people against each other. Just saying.

I don't necessarily mean anything about people judging others here, just the whole "divide and conquer" mentality that cults use to isolate people from their friends and family and into their cult, and most religions indulge in. I can't stand how some people need to feel so superior to others. No one is superior to anyone else, no matter what their beliefs or opinions are. You know, the whole "We're better than them because *we* believe this way, and they don't" mentality.

Over the centuries people who misunderstood or misinterpreted the Bible have done terrible things. The Bible has been misused to defend bloody crusades and tragic inquisitions; to support slavery, apartheid, and segregation; to persecute Jews and other non-Christian people of faith; to support Hitler's Third Reich and the Holocaust; to oppose medical science; to condemn interracial marriage; to execute women as witches; and to support the Ku Klux Klan.

We'd like to believe that no person of good will would misuse the Bible to support his or her prejudice. But time and time again it has happened with tragic results.

Shakespeare said it this way: "Even the Devil can cite Scripture for his purpose."

God bless all the real Christians in my life, and to all the other Right Wing judgmental bunch out there, well, hope you all find Jesus!

I just really thought about the whole Chk-Fil-A thing, what with all those people flocking like sheep to show their enthusiasm to support hate and intolerance, and it occurred to me that that is no different than the way mobs used to act in the past when it came to lynchings, or even further back when it came to witch burnings!

Seriously, what the fuck is wrong with people?!

If you care anything at all about what *true* free speech means, you would make a stand of your own and unfriend anyone you know of that supports such ignorance, whether you're gay or not. Something to think about.

I just wonder, if it was on the news that people were flocking to some fast food restaurant to show their support of making sure that black people couldn't have the same rights as everyone else, would it then be considered "religious freedom" and "freedom of speech"?

I would hope not! And what's going on now is no different! Bigotry is bigotry no matter how it's presented or packaged, and it makes me sick that in this day and age it still exists.

Got to love how the Right Wing nuts flock to some fast food restaurant to show support, and in defense say it's because they are sick and tired of others trying to take away their freedoms, yet they don't see how *they* are trying to take away freedom from other people. Wow.

"If you're against gay marriage don't enter into a gay marriage. Two men marrying would have absolutely no effect on your marriage so why does *your* moral code have to dictate my life? And using the Bible to justify it...once people of different races were not allowed to marry, and once we were allowed to *own* other people and good Christian people cited the Bible as justification.

Folks claim the Bible never changes, but how people read and interpret it sure does. Unless there are folks who still think God wants us to own slaves and prevent interracial marriage. Show of hands..."

-Author Mark Allen Gunnells

"Religious controversies are always productive of more acrimony and irreconcilable hatreds than those which spring from any other cause. Of all the animosities which have existed among mankind, those which are caused by the difference of sentiments in religion appear to be the most inveterate and distressing, and ought most to be depreciated. I was in hopes that the enlightened and liberal policy, which has marked the present age, would at least have reconciled Christians of every denomination so far that we should never again see the religious disputes carried to such a pitch as to endanger the peace of society."

-George Washington

And another thing to follow up on: As I've said before, I do not debate religion (or politics, but that's another story all together), but I will say this: For those that want to stick to the belief that homosexuality is wrong because "it says so in the Bible", well, then here's something to think about: the Bible was written by people when they thought the world was flat, and that stoning people to death for committing adultery, killing children for being disobedient, killing people for eating pork (or fish), and owning slaves was alright, all things that we as a society of civilized, intelligent people have realized was wrong and barbaric to think, so why in the *hell* do some people still want to clink to the old "laws" about homosexuality?

A clever way of expressing what I have for years: Sexuality is a natural human function. Repress it, and it warps, twists, and mutates. And then it's expressed in harmful, unhealthy ways.

I really don't understand why society feels such a need to place labels on everything. Sure, some people are either "gay", "straight", or "bi", but some people simply like having sex, and just because they do it with someone of the same (or different) sex doesn't mean they are of a particular sexual orientation - it simply means they enjoyed having sex with a person.

Example: If I were to have sex with a woman today, that does not mean I am now "straight". It means I wanted to be a lesbian for a day, kidding. Seriously, though, it would only mean I enjoyed having sex with a woman. And the same applies for any straight man who either gets a blow job from, or fucks (to put it bluntly) another man. Simple.

People need to get over themselves. Who cares if two guys or two girls get married and adopt kids? They are the ones saving a child from being in foster care, which is awesome. And when people bring the Bible into it, who 100% lives exactly by the Bible? These people need to worry about their own life and not someone else's. Worry about world hunger, or child abuse/neglect, or elderly abuse/neglect, not people who are happily in love and deserve the right to be able to get married.

It makes me so mad that in 2013 everyone complains about labeling people, but everyone's so quick to judge but yet yell out only God can judge, blah blah blah. Stop judging people for who they are!

Who knows but if people took the energy they spend on preventing same sex marriage and focused on real issues, and mentored troubled kids, the world would be better, but these people are miserable in their own life and are on a mission to make others miserable. It's sad and plain ignorant.

It blows my mind that some people actually listen to all this "hate" rhetoric from these politicians instead of insisting they focus on important issues, like war, poverty, unemployment, and most importantly the economy. Hmmm, guess it makes more sense to attack homosexuals instead...NOT!

And some people tend to forget all the other old laws of the Bible that we know longer adhere to, like stoning divorced women to death, punishing disobedient children by putting them to death, making a woman marry her rapist -or stoning her to death if she doesn't-, and slavery. All those things are mentioned as "God's Laws" as well, but over time we have come to realize how barbaric they are, so why are we as a people still only clinging to the homosexual thing?

Something I truly hate is when small minded people try to say things to try to sound larger minded than they are, because it just doesn't work! It makes them sound even smaller minded than they already are! Word!

On another note, straight guys don't spend much time thinking about gay sex.
Rick Santorum can't seem to stop.

I'm just saying.

He's like a little rage-a-holic playground bully who is upset because some other kids are getting to do something he wants to but can't!

He has compared homosexuality to incest and called the preservation of traditional marriage "the ultimate homeland security issue".

If he tries to run for President, we should make it a crusade to expose how evil he is. There are no words to describe what a plague he is on society. (But, damn, I think he is sexy as hell, DON'T JUDGE ME!!)

Oh good Lord. I don't know what to say any more. Never argue with an idiot, they will drag you down to their level, then beat you with years of experience!

If some people claim they "chose to be gay" then they probably just said it to get people's attention and were never gay in the first place. Why should it make a difference anyway? People should be allowed to love or marry whoever they want regardless of the gender. Whether it's Adam and Eve, or Adrienne and Eve, or Adam and Steve.

It's funny that they think it's "a choice", but they only support "choosing" heterosexuality. Why not support the right to choose then?

You're born gay and it's not a choice. I hate people like that that think they know what it's like to be gay and how it works. Are you gay? No then you can't say if it's a choice. It's called leaving people alone and letting them live their lives. I mean this is the same situation as racism. People just tend to not like things that are different

Yeah don't you know I woke up one day and said "hmmmm well I think I don't get tortured enough as is, I think I want to make my junior high and high school years pure hell by becoming gay. Yes I'm going to turn gay at 13 even though I've had an obvious attraction to boys since like 5 or 6, you know, but I think I'm going to "turn" gay'................................. Some people are fucking dumb.

I certainly can't speak for anyone but myself, but I was *definitely* born gay. I do believe no one was born a hater however, so it seems odd that so-called Christians would choose hate over love. Jesus is crying in Heaven, hypocrites.

Well if we can "choose our sexual orientation" then let us choose to be gay! Flipping homophobes!!

Someone needs to start asking those who think that way the *real* question: When did they choose to be straight? When did they tell their parents that they were straight? Is this a choice that they make every day when they wake up? Do they always make the same choice? Have they ever made the choice to be gay so that they have a better perspective on the entire range of their choices?

If we aren't born this way then why is it that all people on earth aren't straight. If we could have chosen to be straight then wouldn't we have done it already? We have to face difficulties every day because of who we are and we did not choose this. It was the way we were born. You do not have a choice between straight or gay...You only find out later in life when you find love.... AND LOVE IS LOVE NO

MATTER IF YOU ARE TWO MALES, TWO
FEMALES, OR A MAN AND WOMEN COUPLE!!

I don't tolerate ignorance and bigotry in any form!
This is no different than racism! I thought this
goddamn fight was already fought in the 1970's!
Wow.

If you're a Christian who believes that being gay is
a morally reprehensible offense against God, then
you share a mindset, worldview and moral structure
with the kids who hounded Jamey Rodemeyer,
literally, to death. It is your ethos, your convictions
and your theology that informed, supported and
encouraged their cruelty.

It always amazes (and scares) me how a lot of
people in the Red States can sometimes get so violent
and angry when anything "gay" is mentioned or
whatever. People fly into a frothing rage. Pitchforks
are found. Torches become lit. It's just sex, folks; can
we *not* grow up and get the fuck over that fact, yet?
Just saying.

Personally I think that one of the major problems in
our country is that we treat the subject of sex as if it
is so taboo, and act like children ourselves when we
are exposed to it. I think that we should all be taught
at an early age that sex is as natural as using the
bathroom, but that it is something to be very
responsible about, and not something to snicker
about like immature idiots.

About me getting so upset with some people "for
disagreeing with me", well, it's not about someone

disagreeing with me, say on something about a movie, a band, or any other type entertainment, or even politics, this is something where someone is telling me that they do not believe I as a fellow human being have the right to live my life in peace, and not be discriminated against.

It would be the same as someone who is black (or Jewish, or any other ethnicity) having someone tell them that they are wrong for being who they are. That is just so wrong in so many ways.

As for people disagreeing with me, hell, I welcome it! Matter of fact, I love having friends with diverse opinions that differ with mine, and would find it to be a very boring world if everyone thought the same was as I do - except on this one matter!

To say that we, as modern Americans, currently live by the "traditional" definition of marriage is to ignore history. Up until a few hundred years ago, marriage was not based entirely on the romantic love of one man and one woman. Over the past 6,000 years of recorded history, the institution of marriage has been used to unite nations, end wars, and build and gather wealth. Such arrangements span all continents and cultures. In fact, if you really want to see examples of a "traditional" marriage, you should be looking to India, where many of the wealthier families still arrange marriages for their children.

But guess I should assume that, in his profound ignorance, Mr. Cathy was using the word "traditional" as a synonym for "biblical". Well, if this is the case, then Mr. Cathy is obviously as ignorant of the Bible as he is the history of the institution of marriage. The sanctity of marriage, as described by the Bible, has been corrupted for hundreds of years now. Based on the stories and the laws recorded in The Bible, there are twelve basic and explicit rules regarding marriage:

~ Marriage consists of one man and one or more than one woman (Gen 4:19, 4:23, 26:34, 28:9, 29:26-30, 30:26, 31:17, 32:22, 36:2, 36:10, 37:2, Ex. 21:10, Judges 8:30, 1 Sam 1:2, 25:43, 27:3, 30:5, 30:18, 2 Sam 2:2, 3:2-5, 1 Chron 3:1-3, 4:5, 8:8, 14:3, 2 Chron 11:21, 13:21, 24:3).

~ Nothing prevents a man from taking on concubines or sexual slaves in addition to the wife or wives he may already have (Gen 25:6, Judges 8:31, 2 Sam 5:13, 1 Kings 11:3, 1 Chron 3:9, 2 Chron 11:21, Dan 5:2-3).

~ A man might choose any woman he wants for his wife (Gen 6:2, Deut 21:11), provided only that she is not already another man's wife (Lev 18:14-16, Deut. 22:30) or a relative (Lev 18:11, 20:17, Lev 20:14, Lev 18:18).

~ The concept of a woman giving her consent to being married is not in the Bible.

If a woman cannot be proven to be a virgin at the time of marriage, she shall be stoned to death (Deut 22:13-21).

~ A rapist must marry his victim (Ex. 22:16, Deut. 22:28-29), unless she was already a fiancé, in which case he should be put to death if he raped her in the country, but both of them killed if he raped her in town (Deut. 22:23-27).

~ If a man dies childless, his brother must marry the widow (Gen 38:6-10, Deut 25:5-10, Mark 12:19, Luke 20:28).

~ Women must marry the man of their father's choosing (Gen. 24:4, Josh.15:16-17, Judges 1:12-13, 12:9, 21:1, 1 Sam 17:25, 18:19, 1 Kings 2:21, 1 Chron 2:35, Jer 29:6, Dan 11:17).

~ Women are the property of their fathers until married and the property of their husbands thereafter (Ex. 20:17, 22:17, Deut. 22:24, Mat 22:25).

~ The value of a woman might be approximately seven years' work (Gen 29:14-30).

~ Inter-faith marriages are prohibited (Gen 24:3, 28:1, 28:6, Num 25:1-9, Ezra 9:12, Neh 10:30, 2 Cor 6:14).

~ Divorce is forbidden (Deut 22:19, Matt 5:32, 19:9, Mark 10:9-12, Luke 16:18, Rom 7:2, 1 Cor 7:10-11, 7:39).

~ It is better to not get married at all—although marriage is not a sin (Matt 19:10, I Cor 7:1, 7:27-28, 7:32-34, 7:38).

Many of these biblical traditions and laws are considered barbaric (and even criminal) now, yet this is how the Bible defines marriage in its text.

But perhaps Mr. Cathy uses the word "Biblical" to describe the Bible's few passages that seem to outlaw homosexual relations, of which the most often quoted are in Leviticus. This too shows his profound ignorance and hypocrisy, as Leviticus is rife with "laws" that he and so many others ignore.

Does Mr. Cathy advocate that no one be allowed to sow their fields with two different types of grain or wear clothing made of two different types of thread (Lev. 19:19)? Does Mr. Cathy believe that people with disabilities are unfit to worship God (Lev. 21:17-18)? Does Mr. Cathy abhor men who round their hair at the temples or mar the edges of their beards (Lev. 19:27)?

Moreover, why does Chick-fil-A sponsor a Bowl game every year, despite the Bible's warnings against touching the carcass of a pig (Lev. 11:8) and the presence of cheerleaders for men to lust after (a violation of the Tenth Commandment)? For that matter, why does Chick-fil-A serve sausage and bacon, which is also considered unclean (Lev. 11:8)?

The answer is simple: the "laws" in Leviticus are not Commandments handed down by God, but the words of men, created to preserve and protect the fledgling Jewish tribes. Mr. Cathy and others cherry-pick from the Bible to justify their fear of and hatred for homosexuals, just as others once did to justify slavery.

So in the end, I am left knowing that Mr. Cathy and Chick-fil-A don't support the "traditional", "biblical" institution of marriage, but instead, they support institutionalized hate. Moreover, in giving money to organizations that advocate against same-sex marriage, Mr. Cathy and Chick-fil-A support the suspending the 14th Amendment Rights of homosexuals.

I understand that Chick-fil-A stated in a press release that it does not discriminate against homosexual patrons or employees, but that is only because it is illegal to openly do so. Mr. Cathy's words have betrayed his true feelings—he is a bigot—and no amount of tasty food will change that fact.

I have friends and family members who are homosexuals—these are people that I love and respect. They want nothing but the freedom to love those that they wish to love and live their lives in peace. Yet Mr. Cathy wishes to prevent this. I cannot in good conscience continue to eat at Chick-fil-A knowing that the profits from each meal will, in part, go to funding the bigotry that Mr. Cathy, Chick-fil-A, and WinShape support. For those reasons, I will no longer support Chick-fil-A with my patronage.

Everyone has the right to their own opinion. But NO ONE has the right to use their own opinion as a justification for denying other people rights. No one is cramming their opinion down someone else's throat when they highlight someone's bigotry. If you oppose equal rights for a certain group of people, you are a bigot. It's not an opinion, it's a fact based on the definition of the word "bigot".

Yes, you do have the right to be a bigot, but you don't have the right to not be called out on it. Just because you can have any opinion doesn't mean people have to respect it.

If the CEO of Chik-Fil-A came out and said he dislikes beef, that'd be one thing. Totally his opinion, which everyone is entitled to. But when it comes out that not only does he dislike beef, but he actually donates money to groups that go around slaughtering and burning up cows everywhere so they can't be consumed - if you're a fan of burgers, would you be outraged?

Nothing gripes my ass more than when I see some ignorant person on TV, nodding as they talk in their slower-than-hell Southern drawl accent, as if they are an authority on what they are talking about when in all honesty they don't know jack shit and should shut the fuck up! And they cite shit they believe is in the Bible, like "traditional marriage", when if they took time and actually *read* the fucking thing, they would see that they don't have a fucking clue what is actually described as "traditional marriage" in there.

Is it a lost cause to get through to the Christians who oppose gay marriage that their opinions and their beliefs don't matter? It is a civil rights issue. If you believe that it's not okay with your God, then don't marry someone of the same sex! But for God's sake, allow others the opportunity to live without interference from your religious beliefs. You do you, don't police everyone else into living by your antiquated religious rules. Do we not all have free will? How is it people are so self absorbed they can't comprehend this?

For the record, there are also *lots* of other "abominations" in the Bible that we no longer adhere to as a society, things like stoning women to death for divorcing their husbands, or putting unruly outspoken children to death, or killing someone for eating pork, or making women marry their rapists.

I do so seriously wish people would *read* their fucking Bible before quoting from it.

No matter how much I may disagree with or dislike any particular religion, I have respect for everyone's religion, and I just wish that people of certain religions offered the same respect to other people in return. Just saying.

If you censor yourself when it comes to someone else's ignorance, you're allowing that ignorance to continue and possibly grow. When you speak up, you're encouraging other people with similar views to speak up as well.

I certainly don't believe in censoring myself either. But there is such a thing as being tactful and not being an obnoxious jerk about it.

I don't really care if people agree with me or not, I just hope that I can make them *think*!

To everyone who is boohooing that their rights are being stripped away, using the "They took God and prayer out of schools" argument, well here's the *real deal*: No, they didn't take God and prayer out of schools. If your child wants to sit in his/her classroom and pray quietly to his/her "god", that is *fine*! What isn't fine, and what has changed, is that it is no longer tolerable to enforce class-led prayers, forcing everyone in the class to pray to *one* "god".

So, in other words, this only reinforces the rights of each and every individual in the classroom, NOT TAKING ANYONE'S RIGHTS AWAY! True story. Get it now? I'll give you a few minutes. You're welcome.

What gets me is all these small minded idiotic people who are still against gay rights, and declaring how it's a choice and blah blah blah bullshit bullshit more bullshit, not taking into account how over thousands and thousands of years there have been *millions* of homosexual people on this planet, yet they seem to expect gay people to all of a sudden in this day and age to go:
Oh, it's a sin, and a choice, and against God, and more blah blah bullshit, and then turn straight.

Wow!

People amaze the shit out of me sometimes!

It makes me sick how certain white people think they're the superior race, and want to demean and belittle others because they're different than them. I just watched *Crazy In Alabama* last night, and it makes me ashamed to be white when I see how black people were treated by ignorant, small minded racist bigots!

You know, not to sound too corny or anything, but I think in this day and age, instead of letting each other's differences separate us, we as humans should try reaching out more often and trying to come together and celebrate that we are all unique and different. Just a thought.

PS: About the whole "oh, that's so gay" issue, well, I want to say: Please educate yourselves for the sake of all mankind! I'm not offended because I'm gay, it offends me as an educated person! Yes, the term 'gay' has been used to describe homosexual people, but that doesn't make that the correct meaning either, nor does fag or queer. Matter of fact the term "That is so queer" would be a lot more an appropriate slang since the word queer means odd or weird.

Gay does not now nor never meant *lame*! Lame is the right word for lame, why can't the young people of today educate themselves and use the proper slang? Word!

III.

"Grammar Nazi (aka: Some of my thoughts on Grammar rules)"…

Yes, I'm a Grammar Nazi and proud of it. I am all for wiping out ignorance in this country. I'm sick and tired of people wallowing in their dumbed down state of ignorance, and then getting defensive when someone tries to help them. I believe that people should take pride in their language, and learn how to speak and spell it properly. That's all.

Why do people get so goddamn defensive when someone else tries to help them and correct any spelling errors they make? I don't understand it. I know that I sure do appreciate it if and/or when someone points it out to me. I always find it very helpful! And lord knows I make my share of grammatical errors, and I sure do appreciate it when there is someone to politely point them out. Especially being a writer, I find it most helpful. And especially being an American who prides myself on knowing the English language, I definitely find it most helpful.

I guess one of the reasons I'm so tough on some people when I see grammatical errors is because not only am I a writer, but an editor as well, and it is just habit with me when I read something to automatically want to catch errors and correct them.

It is an involuntary reflex, one I've developed over time. It is something I do to help someone, not to belittle or insult them, not to be condescending in any way.

I self taught myself to be a writer and editor, and I take pride in what I do, and I just have the philosophy that if I can do it, then *anyone* can do it. Biggest pet peeve ever, people typing like they have had no education at all! I should not need a translator to read status updates. Just saying.

By the way, sometimes I say shit on the web just because I like the way the words look when I type them up. As a writer, I love to play around with words, sentences, and sentence structure for the sake of trying to be creative and (hopefully) find my muse.

Sometimes it doesn't have a thing to do with how I personally think or feel about something. And as a writer, I have to explore and use all sorts of the English language, not just the parts some people deem appropriate.

You know, whenever someone tells me I use certain words they consider "bad", I think of Annie Wilkes from the movie *Misery*, and when she made Paul Sheldon burn his book because it had swear words in it! People, they're only words, please grow up already!

You know, I'm curious, why is it that anyone who is put off by horrendous misspelling is called Grammar Nazi and made fun of, yet the ignorant motherfuckers who post on the Internet and don't know the difference between "your" and "you're", "then" and "than", or "their", "there" and "they're" get defended? Wow! What the fuck is society coming to?

Oh, for the record, "Cause" and "Because" are two different words. True story.

Example: I couldn't donate to their cause because I was light on funds.

Now, here's the wrong way: I couldn't donate to their cause cause I was light on funds.

See the difference? Hope so.

(Ok, sure, you can say "cause" in place of "because" if you put an apostrophe in front, like this: 'cause. But I'm noticing a *lot* of people aren't doing that. Hell, I was one of them until just recently, but luckily I've learned the error of my ways.)

Something that I've just recently discovered that bothers the hell out of me is that it seems that for several years some people have been mistakenly putting punctuation marks inside quotation marks when it's not dialogue. And there are some people who declare that it's right.

Well, it's not! Just because we have been doing something for a long time doesn't make it right. People in general go by a "frame of reference", meaning how they grew up and what they have always known and believed in. And that frame of reference only works until someone stands up and says: Well, that is just wrong and makes no sense at all.

And it makes *no* sense at all to put a punctuation inside a quotation mark alongside a movie or book title unless the punctuation mark is part of the title!

Seriously, as a writer, I would think that would bother the hell out of other writers. I know it does me!

Ok, for anyone who's interested, here is one of the chief reasons I think it is *wrong* to put the punctuation mark inside of quotation marks when it is not dialogue:

The sole reason for putting something in quotes when it isn't dialogue is to highlight a word or a phrase, so if you include the punctuation mark inside of it, you are then ending or interrupting the phrase - or the entire sentence- before it is over.

And as I've stated several times the other reason pertains when it is done with movie, book, song, or album titles, well, ask yourself, is the comma or period part of the title? If not, then why in the hell would it be placed inside quotation marks?!

Seriously, not that hard to realize it is *wrong* to do that! And it seriously distracts the hell out of me when I am reading something, no matter how well written it otherwise is. Debate, discuss, and even argue this point all you want to, but if you are a real lover of the written language, then you would also be as disgusted at this pretentious practice as I am.

Examples:

The sign changed from "Walk," to "Don't Walk," to

"Walk" again within 30 seconds.

See, to me that is only an example of how moronic it looks to put the comma inside the quotation mark, because it interrupts the flow of the entire sentence. When someone puts something in quotes (like air quotes), then it is to highlight that word, then if the sentence continues, the comma should come *after* the quotation, like this:

Examples:

The sign changed from "Walk", to "Don't Walk", to "Walk" again within 30 seconds.

About the grammatical rule of putting punctuation inside of quotation marks when it's not dialogue, well, it's wrong, and I will stand my ground protesting it! I am the 99%!

Yet another reason it is *wrong* to put punctuation inside quotation marks when it isn't dialogue is because it is to distinguish between what is and what isn't dialogue. Simple. When someone puts punctuation inside quotations when it isn't dialogue, it looks confusing, because it looks like dialogue. Understand? Hope so!

To some writers who put punctuation inside quotations when it's not dialogue, especially when referring to one of your book titles, ask yourself this one simple question: Is the punctuation part of the title? If not, then why would you put it inside the quotation marks?

Example: I want to advertise my short story collection "Perfect Strangers."

Should be: I want to advertise my short story collection "Perfect Strangers".
Because the name of the book is "Perfect Strangers" (with no period in the title), not "Perfect Strangers." (with a period in the title).

See what I mean? Hope so. Thank you.

And yet another reason it's wrong to put punctuation inside quotation marks is because it is obvious that some dumbed down lazy buffoon decided to do it because they were too damn lazy and stupid to try to figure out the correct way to do it.

Putting punctuation inside quotation marks when it's not dialogue is something as wrong as people saying "there" in place of "their", or mistaking "your" and "you're".

Especially when it's done with a title of something, like a movie, book, album, etc etc.

All you have to do is ask yourself, is the punctuation part of the title. And if the answer is "NO", then it should only be common sense that it shouldn't go inside the quotation. True story.

And it's something I really wish more people - especially writers and fellow authors- would stand up and speak out about.

Anyways, just wanted to get that out of my system, ha-ha. Thank you!

Look, that's because the U.S. has been so fucking dumbed down it isn't funny! The punctuation goes outside quotation marks unless it's dialogue. If it's not dialogue, the punctuation goes outside the quotation marks. It's really very simple. But as we see, the U.S. are so damn lazy, they decided why try to figure it out when to do it the right way, so just put it inside no matter what. And now all these years later, we have people following suit like sheep.

It's time to change it back to the way it's supposed to be, the right way. Thank you.

About the rule of punctuation and quotation marks, especially when it comes to book or movie titles, simply ask yourself this question:

Does the title have a comma or period (or any other punctuation) in it?

If the answer is no, then it should only stand to reason that you DON'T PUT ONE INSIDE THE QUOTATION MARKS when referring a title.

Simple!

You're welcome!

About how I feel about the rules of grammar and putting punctuation *outside* quotation marks when it's not dialogue continued:

Ok, for everyone who thinks that you should put punctuation inside quotation marks when it's not dialogue (as wrong as that is), here's a question, why don't you just go ahead and put any previous punctuation inside quotation that's preceding what you highlight in quotation marks?

Example:
I love the new Black Sabbath album ",13," and think it's great!

See how ridiculous that looks?!

Well, that's how I (and countless others) think it looks when you put punctuation inside quotation marks when it's not dialogue.

Thank you. Rant now over. Have a good day.

See, what kills me about the people who say, "What does it matter if someone misspells a word (or words) on the internet, it's *only* the Internet, and it's all in fun", is that it *is* on the Internet, and *many* people see it, and then either consciously or unconsciously, they pass the error(s) on.

For example, when someone reads a post with the word "than" wrongly spelled "then", well, if that person is unsure of how the word is spelled correctly, they are more than likely to assume you do, and are going to repeat your mistake - thus further dumbing down the nation.

I have seen this too many times and too many places on the web to know what I'm talking about. Words like "their" and "there" and "then" and "than" (not to count the countless other errors) are popping up all over, but incorrectly spelled - and they are the *only* errors in the post/blog/review I am seeing.

So, I have to ask myself: Why is it that it's *only* a certain set of words that are being erroneously misspelled all over the internet, and by people who otherwise are very literate intellectual people who make no other grammatical errors at all?

It's because after so long, things like that float into the subconscious, and then filter out when least expected.

It sounds crazy, I know, but I am seriously starting to suspect some kind of wild conspiracy to help further dumb down our nation. And that is what I am trying to *stop* when I (politely) point out any errors like I've mentioned. I really wish more people would step up and take part.

So, a message from my heart to all you out there who think "2" means "to" or "too" or "two". (Psst! It's only the *last* one!)

Oh, and don't forget those that confuse "their" and "there", and "you're" and "your", or "than" and "then"! Oh, and let's not overlook the whole "could of" and "should of" instead of the *correct* "could've" and "should've"! I think that is one that drives me bonkers the most! (Yes, remember, it is "could have" or "should have", *not* "could of" or "should of"!!)

It really amazes me just how many people on the web don't know how to spell the simplest of words correctly. I don't mean to sound harsh, but if you don't know how to spell something, all you have to do is either use spell check, or even easier, Google it.

(Trust me, I have to use it quite often!)

It's not like you're sitting in your room by yourself writing in a private journal that only you (and maybe a few friends) will read, this is the world-wide web, where *everyone* around the world can read it. Think about that next time before you post. Just saying.

And, I am going to come get you, tie you down and hobble you, Mr. Man, if you don't quit putting the punctuation mark inside the quotation mark unless it is dialogue! Word!

Thank you, now back to your usual business before I interrupted with my rant here.

Thank you.

-Sincerely, The Grammar Slut ♥ (aka: Proud Grammar Nazi ♥)

IV.

"Children Of Today: My Thoughts On Child-Rearing In Today's World…"

The first thing I usually always hear whenever I voice my opinion on how children should be raised, and/or what I think are some of the major problems with children in this day and age, is that it's easy for me to think (or say) that because I don't have children.

No, spoken like someone who knows that children shouldn't rule the house. Sorry, but that is one of the major problems in this country is too many parents mamby-pamby their children instead of teaching them from a young age that life isn't always about getting your way. It is a known fact that children expect supervision and authority in their lives (even though they may not outwardly want it), and are very confused when it is not present.

I may not have children of my own per say, but I have been just as much a part of my niece and nephew's child rearing to know what I'm talking about. One was raised the way that a vast majority would do it, and the other was raised with more of the type values I am talking about, and guess which one is more successful and career-oriented and responsible, and guess which one is the more "problematic". Don't get me wrong, I love them both equally, and I feel that both my siblings made great parents; it's just that I feel that one had a more successful method than the other.

And, I see that is one of the biggest problems of this nation: the spoiling of and pandering to us all on a grand scheme, that it's sickening, and maddening that more people can't see through it. Well, that's why a piece of shit like some of the most dumbed down movies imaginable gets released because the powers that be know that there are so many mindless people out there like sheep that will go "baa-baa" and go see it because they feel that they better take their whining children or the kids won't love them anymore.

I'm not saying that parents should be like the Grinch, but there are lots of parents that don't allow their children to see some of the garbage that passes for entertainment these days, and they turn out fine, matter of fact, a lot finer than the children that are more "spoiled" and allowed to get their way all the time, and then subsequently be exposed to a lot of garbage being passed off these days as entertainment.

Oh, and about the whole kids being bullies because kids will be kids shit, well…Sorry, but that whole "kids will be kids" defense is the most offensive thing I've ever heard when it comes to defending bullies and bullying!

Yes, there are bullies everywhere, but if people would take damn responsibility and teach their children from a very young age that bullying is wrong, then maybe, just maybe, it would help stop it from occurring (and help stop it from reaching into adulthood). Thank you.

V.

My Stance On Remakes:

It appears that all Hollywood can churn out anymore are god awful sequels and/or horrendous remakes of classics. It isn't that the original films are 'fixed', it is because they get 'stolen'. Why do films need to be remade for anyway? If someone doesn't like the way it looks originally, then move on to another film.

How would you feel if you made a film, then 20 years down the road some unknown filmmaker (or studio) comes along trying to make a name for himself, and decides to do it by remaking your film?!

I agree there have been some really good remakes in film, especially John Carpenter's *The Thing*, David Cronenberg's *The Fly*, and Phillip Kaufman's *Invasion Of The Body Snatchers*. I hate to contradict that when I'm taking my 'stance' against remakes, but the thing is the principal for the remake to begin with: So a whole new generation can appreciate the story, and that, IMO, is wrong, because it robs the original art of filmmaking; and, thus, we see the vision of great film makers like Hitchcock, Welles, Wilder, Capra, DeMille, Polanski, De Palma, Kubrick, Lynch, etc, etc, disappearing from the screen.

Another reason I'm against remakes is I consider it to be thievery on a grand scale. How would all of these popcorn eating fans of these 're-imagined' films feel if they had made the original film themselves just to see some unknown filmmaker wanna-be come along and pilfer their work for their own gain? I don't think they would be too crazy about it then, huh?!

Plus, I consider it to be the same as someone rewriting classic novels, like *To Kill A Mockingbird 2014*, just so someone who doesn't appreciate the way it originally read would read it; you know, dumbing it down so Baby Cakes can understand it! Or could you see someone repainting classic works of art every so many years, like the Mona Lisa, because a whole new generation could "get it"?

As for remakes, I have to admit, even though I take such a stance against remaking films, yes there have been a few that I liked, but I still consider it theft! And it really makes me shudder when it is a film that was originally written *and* directed by the same person, because then when it's remade by someone else it's not a "reinterpretation of the source material"; it is flat out plagiarism!

I see filmmaking as an art, and to me when a work of art is created, we shouldn't want to redo it if the artist doesn't make it up to our liking originally. Fuck that shit! Make them learn to appreciate the original art form, or move onto something new!

Anyways, didn't mean to rant here!

THE END

Randall Brooks is the author of the novels *The Two Worlds of the Mind* and *Von Wyck: The Complete Story By Victor Holocaust*, and three short story collections, *Conversations At The Party*, *Perfect Strangers*, and *The Maze*, as well as his extensive collections of lyrics, *Von Wyck Songbook Volume 1: 1986 - 1988*, *Von Wyck Songbook Volume 2: 1988 - 1991*, *Von Wyck Songbook Volume 3: 1991 - 1997*, and *Von Wyck Songbook Volume 4: 1998 - 2011*.

Brooks has also recently published two collections of his reviews, and a non-fiction book on religion and politics in today's world, *Ranting & Raving*.

He has been writing short stories, lyrical poems, and reviews for several years. His field of choice is psychological erotic satiric mystery suspense.

Even though he has been inspired by a lot of writers over the years (namely Stephen King, Peter Straub, Mary Higgins Clark, and Jackie Collins), he would have to say the biggest inspiration and influence on his writing has been some awesome filmmakers, like Alfred Hitchcock, Brian De Palma, and Stanley Kubrick.

For anyone who's interested in checking out (or reviewing) any of my books, here's the link to my author page on Amazon.com, where you can find everything I've got listed on there in one place.

http://www.amazon.com/Randall-Brooks/e/B005PBWWFK/ref=ntt_athr_dp_pel_1

Thanks for reading!

www.ingramcontent.com/pod-product-compliance
Lightning Source LLC
Chambersburg PA
CBHW070136290526
45789CB00002B/507